W9-BHZ-320

ADVANCED

Reader's Digest

READING skill BUILDER™

PROJECT EDITOR: **WARREN J. HALLIBURTON**

EDITOR: **LINDA BEECH**

CONSULTANTS:

Jorge Garcia, Ed. D.
Supervisor Secondary Reading
Hillsborough County Public
Schools
Tampa, Florida

Susan Pasquini
Reading Specialist /
English Instructor
Escondido High School
San Diego, California

Frank Vernol
Instructional Learning
Secondary Reading
Dallas Independent School
District
Dallas, Texas

Grace Whittaker
Secondary Reading Supervisor
Boston Public Schools
Boston, Massachusetts

Property of
FAMILY OF FAITH
LIBRARY

READER'S DIGEST EDUCATIONAL DIVISION
The credits and acknowledgments that appear on the inside
back cover are hereby made a part of this copyright page.

Reader's Digest ® Trademark Reg. U.S. Pat. Off. Marca Registrada ISBN 0-88300-280-8

□□□ □□□ □□□ Part 1   Reorder No. B32

silver edition

CONTENTS

  Stories for which Audio Lessons are available.

The Other Side of the Mountain

Evans G. Valens

Jill tried to tell her mother what skiing was like. "You're going down and the snow is there and you're all a part of it, kind of, and it's noiseless. You go down and carve nice turns and go into the air and come down and catch and hold. And there's always unknowns. Do I hit the downhill side of this and feel that nice feeling like you do when you do hit the downhill side, or do I hit the flat and go up the other side and bam, the mountain slaps you right in the face, or do I keep control of the mountain and land nicely, and softly, and go on to something else I'm not sure of and then make that, too? The control you have of what's happening is so nice. And it's so gentle. And then at other times coarse and rough and beastly, kind of, and you end up fighting like a dog to stay with it."

Jill was on her way to race in the Snow Cup, the last important race before the Olympic tryouts. Everyone looked upon it as a dress rehearsal. The 1954 U.S. women's Olympic team would undoubtedly come from among Snow Cup contenders. Most sports editors were betting that Jill Kinmont, age 18, would be on that team.

The Snow Cup giant slalom was held in Alta, Utah. Jill arrived a few days early. The air was sharp and cold, and the snow was a lovely, fine dry powder that would spin and sparkle into the air if you merely gave it a swipe with your ski pole. Jill made several runs. The racecourse was a mile and a quarter long and fairly steep. The competitors helped pack it and then skied down alongside, stopping to study each hump and curve and each pair of flags, sometimes sidestepping

A scene from the movie

back up to replot their lines. The first two-thirds of the course, except for a very tight, steep start, was set on a fast, open slope along the west side of Rustler Mountain. Then, above a gully known as the Corkscrew, the course squeezed left through a grove of trees where it lifted suddenly over a 4-foot (1.22-meter) rise, ran across a short plateau and fell precipitously down toward the Alta Lodge on the narrow valley floor. The sharp

bump above the Corkscrew was obviously the spot to watch, a stark test of skill and strength and perhaps of daring. It would be impossible not to go into the air, and it would take some pretty spectacular skiing to make time on that section of the run. But it was just another racing problem as far as Jill was concerned. Jill stopped above the Corkscrew to study the bump, and she had lots of company. The race was going to be won or lost right here.

Jill liked the course and she liked the mountain and she was skiing well. She knew that she could win. Everything would have to go right. If something happened, she wouldn't make it. But it was possible.

Jack Reddish, a Salt Lake skier and Olympic veteran whom Jill had once met, stopped her on her way over to the lodge. "Just bought your picture," he said.

"What do you mean?"

"On the front of *Sports Illustrated.*"

"No!" Jill had expected to see herself in the magazine, but certainly not on the cover.

The January 31 issue of *Sports Illustrated* had nothing on the cover but the name of the magazine, the date and price, and a gorgeous color photograph of Jill Kinmont in a yellow sweater with skis on her shoulder. Inside was a three-page article called "Apple Pie in Sun Valley" with eight photographs. Jill skiing. Jill chatting. Jill in the warming hut. Jill puffing into a ski mitten.

The women's race was scheduled before the men's, as usual. Jill was not at all nervous in the starting gate, although she wanted to get going. At the last moment Jill looked over at Dave McCoy, her friend and ski teacher. He winked and gave her the high sign. She felt as if she owned the world, or would very shortly.

Jill started with a surge of power, crouched low in the straightaway, and then barreled down through the fast, swooping turns on the upper part of the course with a wind at her back. The snow was faster than she'd expected, and she found herself low on a gate, slipping still lower and nearly falling as she struggled to hang onto the hill.

She had recovered by the time she shot down toward the trees and the left turn above the Corkscrew where she had always checked during practice. This time she did not check

because she had already decided that the racer who let his skis run here was likely to win. She got ready to prejump the 4-foot (1.22-meter)-high knoll, but she was moving too fast and started her jump two or three seconds late. So instead of prejumping, she lifted just where the snow surface itself rose up to the stubby plateau.

She had flung herself high into the air and was flying . . . off balance and aware only of the blur of trees coming up at her from below. She fought to get forward over her skis and raised one arm to protect her face from being smashed against the tree trunks. She missed the trees and screamed at two spectators who were now directly in her path. She crashed onto the snow, slid and spun and tumbled another 50 feet (15.24 meters) and slammed into one of the spectators, carrying him on down the hill, thrashing and cartwheeling. In the middle of this final tumble, Jill felt within her body a sudden dull vibration. Except that there was no sound, and there was no pain.

When she stopped sliding she had the odd feeling that parts of her were somehow not connected. She thought maybe this is the way you die.

But she saw vaguely familiar faces and said, "Oh . . . what have I done? I can't move. I don't know what's the matter and I'm scared." She started to sob and thought, *Oh, no . . . here go the Olympic tryouts and everything!*

The ski patrol arrived with a toboggan. Several skiers lifted her with great care—just enough so that the Stokes litter could be slid beneath her. Jill said with some alarm, "I can't feel you touching me!" Something, she now knew, had made her unable to move or feel with most of her body. Whatever this something might be, she wondered if it might keep coming up, whether it would come up still higher, into her head. "I can't feel," she cried again.

Dave went with Jill in the ambulance to Salt Lake, but all Jill thought about was staying awake. She was convinced that she would die if she didn't. She said aloud, "Don't let me go to sleep because I know I won't wake up."

She had other worries, however, the moment she was wheeled into Emergency at the Salt Lake General Hospital.

The doctor began poking her with a pin, saying, "Can you feel this . . . can you feel this?"

Movie reenactment of the fatal fall

"No," she said, again and again and again.

The world that was beginning to close in about her was made of a white ceiling and lavender tubes of light and a swarm of horribly serious faces and a vague, floating medley of disembodied voices that didn't go with the faces.

In Salt Lake City that Sunday evening the first hospital bulletin listed Jill's condition as critical, and stated that "early X-rays indicated the upper portion of Miss Kinmont's back has been fractured." About this time Jill was being wheeled in to surgery.

The operation was a long one and it ended with the boring of two shallow holes in the top of her skull.

When they wheeled her out, she saw Dave hunkering outside the door. He stood up,

that left Jill motionless on the mountain and paralyzed from the neck down

looking worn and gray. She said, "Hi," and he smiled momentarily. She traveled far, far down the hall, and her mother and father were there and she said, "Hi, Mom. Hi, Dad." The next thing she remembered was a number of very small, pink ballerinas, some of them dancing and some just floating in the air.

She slept until morning, and when she awoke she felt as if she were drifting away somewhere. She was vaguely worried but couldn't follow the thought long enough to make anything of it, and when her parents came to see her she was relatively cheerful. She was also an impressive spectacle as she lay in traction, face up and motionless with wide bandages at the back of her neck. A bottle-fed tube ran into a vein in her left arm. Another tube ran from a suction pump into her nose and down her throat. An oxygen tank, with a mask dangling from it, stood close to her head. She was meanwhile being stretched lengthwise by steel tongs which had been fitted into the holes bored into her skull; 35 pounds (15.88 kilograms) of sausage-shaped iron weights hung from a cable which ran over a pulley behind her head and was wired to the tongs. She was lying on a Stryker frame, a canvas-covered metal frame supported at the head and foot by a kind of axle which allowed her to be turned regularly like a roast on a spit. Two hours face up, two hours face down. In the latter position, an opening in the canvas gave her an unobstructed view of the floor.

Jill's condition was still critical. She felt no particular pain except that the back of her neck was stiff and swollen. She didn't even have a headache. Slight feeling had returned to her arms—a vague, tingling awareness—but she had no sensation whatever in her body below the shoulders. The tongs biting into her head were no more painful than a deep scratch, but whenever she thought about the way they were hooked into her skull she began to feel sick.

When Jill awakened Tuesday morning her room was so full of flowers that it looked like a funeral parlor. Five stacks of letters and telegrams were piled against the wall, plus two packages, each of which contained a stuffed animal. It was a very Christmas-like morning.

The Junior Chamber of Commerce, which had sponsored the Snow Cup, donated the gate receipts from the race to help meet hospital expenses.

"I thought I had insurance!" Jill said.

"You did," her father answered.

"Well . . .?"

"Well, it wasn't quite enough, honeygirl."

The local radio station broadcast special Jill Kinmont bulletins, and the stores in town were putting out collection jars labeled HELP JILL UP THE HILL. The money was for the Far West Ski Association's Jill Kinmont Fund.

News clippings about the accident were many and varied although the choice of adjectives to modify the subject was somewhat limited: Jill Kinmont, the plucky young skier . . . The spunky 18-year-old Bishop, California blonde . . . The spunky little lass . . . Plucky Jill Kinmont . . . A spunky young woman . . . Spunky Jill Kinmont . . . Plucky Jill . . .

Jill said, "Isn't it funny, Mom, the way they write these articles?"

The accounts of the accident were constantly surprising. Her flight through the air was never less than 50 feet (15.24 meters) and in one newspaper it reached 100 feet (30.48 meters). Her speed had doubled, she had crashed into everything from tree trunks to whole crowds of spectators, and she had "practically won the race" several times.

Officially, Jill's condition had improved from critical to poor, and everything seemed to be looking up. The oxygen tank and the suction machine were still there, but both appeared to be unnecessary. Intravenous

A helpless Jill Kinmont being carried from accident scene as shown in movie

feeding was a thing of the past. The orthopedic surgeon had offered some very optimistic remarks about the future.

Another doctor wasn't so encouraging. "I don't want to frighten you," he said in a frighteningly subdued voice, "but I must tell you that the mortality rate for this type of injury is very high." He paused uneasily, as if about to speak again, but he only licked his lips. And then he left.

Life seemed to have two levels that were scarcely connected. On one was the sun-tanned skier laughing and worrying about how her hair could be washed with those tongs sunk in her head. On another level was a patient whose body could scarcely function and whose chances of dying, statistically at any rate, were excellent.

On Thursday, four days after the accident, the reporters were let in. The swirl of activity was a circus and a maelstrom. It was quite something to be queen again, even if you had to be stretched out motionless on a slab to make it. But it was disturbing to be asked questions that the questioners seemed to have answered already for themselves.

"How often do you ask yourself, why did it have to happen to me?"

"I never thought of it."

"Were you really going 60 miles (96.54 kilometers) an hour?"

"Twenty-five or 30 is more like it."

"How can you take it just lying there and still smile?"

"How long till you'll be skiing again?"

Bill Kinmont, Jill's dad,

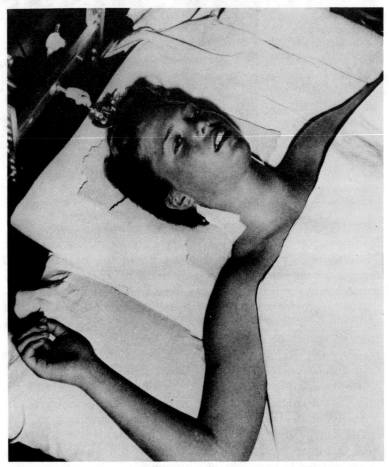

Her neck in traction, her prognosis discouraging, Jill wonders about her future.

called in another doctor, a friend of his, Ted Lynn, from Los Angeles.

Dr. Lynn flew up the next day. He examined Jill, checked her records and X rays, and summarized the situation matter-of-factly. She had sustained a fracture-dislocation of the spine at the level of the fourth, fifth and sixth cervical vertebrae, resulting in transection of the cord. In other words, the spinal cord was completely severed low in the neck, which caused permanent paralysis, both motor and sensory, below the shoulders. No movement, no feeling. Breathing remained unimpaired, however, and the arms might retain some function.

It was difficult to account for all the vague optimism that had been wafted about the hospital throughout the week, for these facts were already on record, having been directly observed during the operation. At that time the spinal cord was seen to be mashed to a pulp and there was no continuity of the structure. Nor could anything possibly be done to restore it. Jill had been paralyzed from the shoulders down since the moment of impact.

Jill, for her own part, had not yet had time to worry about the future. It was enough to worry about now and an hour from now. Also, she had been busy with visitors and letters. She was aware that she might never race again, but the greatest disappointment was that she was already missing the Olympic tryouts. No one had yet suggested to her that she might not be walking again at some vaguely future time.

If the break had been a fraction of an inch lower, she would have had full use of her hands. And of course, if she had slowed down, then she wouldn't have crashed at all.

And if she'd thought other competitors would slow down there, then she would have taken the time to slow down also. But she had decided to win.

If, if, if, if, . . . is a good game and any number can play and anything whatever can be pretended. If the break had been a fraction of an inch higher she could not have breathed without an iron lung. If just this or that thing had been different, she would be dead. Life is a million ifs a day. But if only you had your hands you could be practically independent.

In May Jill was allowed to sit up most of the day, which was wonderful because she could at last scratch her own nose whenever she wished. She spent two hours a day with a physical therapist.

Dr. Lynn also arranged for John Campbell to come and see what he could do in the way of spoons and forks and pens. Campbell was an occupational therapist and a most inventive designer of braces and devices.

"So there's no reason why you can't eat and write and brush your teeth and make up your face," John Campbell said. "If we can just figure how to manage it."

He had some ideas, but meanwhile he put her to work

weaving a white-and-orange pot holder. Jill thought this might be fun, but every time she shoved the shuttle between the threads she had to make dozens of futile attempts before she could grab hold of it again. The task was so frustrating and her arms became so painfully tired that tears started flowing down her cheeks. She began sobbing and couldn't stop. Then she got hotly angry at herself for acting so childishly and this made her cry even harder.

Days and days later she did finish the pot holder. It came out scraggly and shaped like an hourglass.

Jill's handwriting was improving and by the first week in June she was printing letters half an inch (1.27 centimeters) high. She composed a birthday poem for her mother.

Jill had been hospitalized for more than five months, and everything that could be done for her medically had been done. Her legs had lost some flesh recently but her weight had stabilized at 120 pounds (54.43 kilograms) only ten pounds (4.54 kilograms) less than it had been in January. She no longer required the constant presence of a nurse, but she would always need help dressing and moving herself bodily in and out of her chair.

Physically, then, her future was more or less predictable and there was no indecision about what had to be done. In every other way, however, it was like looking out over a trackless and gloomy moor. No horizons were visible and the view in every direction was equally murky.

Jill dreamed at night that she was skiing and that she had everything in her life under control. She stopped and reached down to release her binding. The moment she stepped off her skis she was in a wheelchair.

But she was tired of being known as Jill Kinmont, the girl who might have been the greatest thing on a pair of boards. She had once been interesting to people because she had really been something on skis. From now on people were not going to find her interesting for the old familiar reasons.

So, was there some other answer or some new direction? Probably. Maybe. Jill had no idea what it might be. She felt very sorry for herself. Then she became angry at herself for allowing herself to feel this way.

A bravely smiling Jill being pushed in her ski-equipped wheelchair by her former coach, Dave McCoy.

Jill went to UCLA and got her college degree. Then she registered for several postgraduate courses she felt would be helpful to her as a teacher.

One day on campus Jill heard about a young man named Bill Judd who was in a wheelchair and was teaching at a place called the Clinic School. She looked up Clinic School in the UCLA bulletin and found that it was run by the university's Psychology Department. It was for boys between the ages of 9 and 14 who were of average or above average intelligence but who nevertheless were unable to keep up with their elementary or high school classes. The school was staffed by several instructors and by students enrolled in a course concerned with learning disorders.

Jill telephoned the school and was referred to a Mr. Jenson. "This is Jill Kinmont," she said. "The school bulletin says you offer a training course where the students work right in the classroom with the children. Now . . ." She took a long breath. "The School of Education won't accept me because of my handicap. I would like to know if you would accept me for the summer session."

Mr. Jenson replied, "I don't know why not."

Jill liked the Clinic School from the first session. She was one of four psychology students working two hours a day with a class of 15 boys.

One sunny morning immediately after Jill's class in learning disorders, Mr. Jenson came in to say that there would be a job opening for a regular teacher at the Clinic School next semester. Jill went to see him the following day to say she wanted to apply. The Clinic School had been pleased with her work; she had plenty of drive and asked for no favors, and she had a sense of respect for children that made the difference between teaching and merely instructing. Mr. Jenson said she would have to make an official application, but there would be no difficulty about her getting the job.

Jill wheeled out of the building and stopped her chair as soon as she found herself alone on a quiet path. She leaned her head far back in her chair, stretching with joy and relief, and closed her eyes. She felt as if spring sunlight were beaming on her after a gray winter.

Jill is still asked occasionally to describe the nearly fatal accident. She always begins, "It was a beautiful morning and the snow was like velvet..." A friend asked her if she still thought about skiing. She was silent for a while and then she said, "When I'm alone with myself and it's absolutely quiet, I can feel what it's like, skiing. I can still remember the runs—every slalom course, every downhill—and in my mind I can still feel where I want to prejump and where I'll have to check. I know I could still ski . . . if I could ski."

Number of Words: 3610 ÷ _____ Minutes Reading Time = Rate _____

I. CHARACTERIZATION

Put a check √ in front of the five words that could be used to describe Jill Kinmont. Be able to support your answers with information given in the story.

_____ **1.** greedy   _____ **6.** conceited

_____ **2.** courageous   _____ **7.** competitive

_____ **3.** vivacious   _____ **8.** independent

_____ **4.** reckless   _____ **9.** practical

_____ **5.** self-pitying   _____ **10.** timid

6 points for each correct answer   SCORE: _____

II. INFERENCES

Circle the letter of the best answer for each question.

1. What was the "sudden dull vibration" that Jill felt as she tumbled down the hill?
   a. her skis coming off
   b. a slender tree snapping
   c. her spine being fractured

2. How accurate were the newspaper accounts of Jill's accident?
   a. The facts were distorted and grossly exaggerated.
   b. Jill was unjustly blamed for being too reckless.
   c. Most were fine examples of on-the-spot reporting.

3. What is the meaning of the statement "Life is a million 'ifs' a day"?
   a. Most people face danger every day of their lives.
   b. People's lives are often determined by uncontrollable circumstances.
   c. Most people wouldn't want to live if they could see the future.

4. What was the greatest obstacle that Jill had to overcome?
   a. learning how to use the parts of her body that had no feeling
   b. accepting the fact the she would never ski again
   c. building a productive life in spite of her handicap

10 points for each correct answer   SCORE: _____

III. AUTHOR'S PURPOSE

Circle the letter of the best ending for each sentence.

1. The author's purpose in writing this story is to
   a. share a personal experience with the reader.
   b. show how human beings can survive the worst tragedies.
   c. show how taking risks can lead to tragedy.

2. The author emphasizes the plight of the main character by
   a. showing how much skiing meant to her.
   b. describing how other people pitied her.
   c. showing how she would have to spend the rest of her life in a wheelchair.

3. The author obviously feels that Jill's life is
   a. an example of the worst that can happen to someone.
   b. not as good as it might have been, but still worthwhile.
   c. an inspiration to all who might give up hope.

10 points for each correct answer   SCORE: _____

PERFECT TOTAL SCORE: 100   TOTAL SCORE: _____

IV. QUESTIONS FOR THOUGHT

What qualities do you think a person must possess in order to handle a "hopeless" situation the way Jill did? Why?

Getting Along with Glenn

Bill Conklin

In the advertising agency where I work as a copywriter, the word has long since gone around that I am vaguely daffy. It's true. I rarely say what I mean. I'm a lad who becomes involved in impossible situations. I quite literally get into things. (For example, a lamp shade once got stuck on my head in the middle of a rather exciting meeting.) And things have worsened steadily since Glenn Gordon came in as creative head of our agency.

The first time Glenn ever saw me was the day actor Gregory Peck toured our offices, gathering background for a movie role. At that moment I was in the art department, waiting for an artist friend to return from lunch. Sitting at a drawing board, idly drawing rectangles, I suddenly looked up to see Glenn Gordon, Gregory Peck and other important folk filing into the room. Sizing up the situation quickly, I did what I maintain was the right thing. Glenn Gordon was there to show Mr. Peck artists. I became one. I drew rectangles furiously.

"This is what we call the bull pen," Glenn said. "Here our rough ideas are rendered into finished layouts to show clients." He smiled at the artists in the bull pen. He smiled at me. Gregory Peck smiled at me. I smiled back.

As soon as they departed, I determined not to wait around for the artist any longer. I scribbled a memorandum for him to call me, took a short cut to my office and spun a piece of copy paper into my typewriter. Shadows fell across my opaque-glass cubicle, voices murmured, and I glanced up, appalled. There were Glenn Gordon, Gregory Peck, the others.

"This is a typical copywriter's office," Glenn began. "Here, basic copy is pre—" He stared at me and his mouth gaped, caught on a syllable.

I smiled at him. I smiled at Gregory Peck. The group proceeded on and I returned to my current assignment, but my heart wasn't in it. The battle was joined. I knew with a dread certainty that Glenn and I would meet in the lists again.

Sure enough. A week later a secretary had her purse stolen. Presuming it taken by a transient messenger and hoping at least to recover the bag, she asked me to search the waste-basket in the men's room. I went in and began looking through the big basket. Glenn Gordon entered. It didn't occur to me that he had no idea why I was examining crumpled paper towels in the lavatory of a hundred-million-dollar advertising agency. I saw it only as a good time to explain the Peck incident.

I emerged from the basket and ventured, "About Gregory Peck, sir. I wasn't twins the other day. I was in the art department to see about cutting up some horses." (It didn't come out right, as usual, but I had been there that day to get some horse photos trimmed and mounted.) Glenn executed a few backward steps, smiling pacifically, and bolted out the door.

After that, things went smoothly until the day we came face to face in the production department. Glenn motioned me to a chair. Obviously he needed to know more about me and, remarkably, I was more than equal to the occasion. We sat calmly together, and chatted easily about a variety of things. As we talked, Glenn became visibly relieved.

I decided to quit while I was ahead. I stood up quickly and leaned toward Glenn to say

good-by. A simple "So long" or "Nice talking with you" would have sufficed. But as I searched for the appropriate farewell, my mind (never very stable) gave way completely. No words came. Glenn, having no inkling that I meant to leave, unable to understand why I was suddenly towering over him silently, froze like a frightened rabbit.

My mouth began to move wordlessly; finally I managed to croak. "Me go now," I said hoarsely and walked away.

Why I said that—like most of the things I do—had an explanation, but it's the kind that invariably leads to still more confusion. I had been reading about the late humorist Robert Benchley. Once, during a bad play involving a character who spoke pidgin English, Benchley had said "Me go" and had left the theater. I suppose that the phrase stuck in my subconscious until that unfortunate moment and then tumbled out to help do me in.

Soon there was another incident. The time, 4:20 p.m. of a hectic day. I had just escaped from a meeting where I had warmly shaken hands with a colleague at the agency instead of with the client. I was headed for the 11th floor and the sanctuary of my own office, where I often have things in control. The elevator door opened and there was Glenn Gordon. He smiled resolutely and said, "Hi, there, how are you?"

I stepped aboard and answered, "Hi! Just getting back from lunch?"

Convene all the authors of all the articles on how to succeed in business. Ask them to select the one phrase *not* to be uttered to the boss at twenty past four in the afternoon. "Just getting back from lunch?" would score an enthusiastic victory by acclamation. Do believe me, that isn't what I meant to say. I meant to say something else. Exactly *what,* I really do not know.

That was Tuesday. Wednesday was worse. I took a late lunch and celebrated a crisp January day in Manhattan by buying my fiancée a huge stuffed poodle. On my way back I saw a pair of earrings I thought she would like and bought those, too.

It was midafternoon when I returned to my cubicle. Sitting there, my quixotic mind far from advertising, I had an ingenious idea—I decided to put the earrings on the dog's ears and thus bestow both presents with an original touch. I unwrapped the cumbersome poodle and hoisted it up onto my desk. Carefully I took a floppy ear in my hand and began fas-

tening a gold, bell-shaped earring to it.

Fate was tempted; fate replied. As I bent earnestly to my task, Glenn Gordon came down the aisle and glanced in my office. Everywhere about me dedicated copywriters were creating unforgettable phrases. Typewriters were singing the praises of myriad products—I was putting earrings on a stuffed poodle. I realize now it must have been, on top of everything else, almost a traumatic experience for Glenn. I grinned a foolish grin and said hollowly, "Dog."

In movies and plays I have often seen and admired a well-executed double take. Glenn performed not one, not two, but three takes. He stared, opened his mouth to speak, then rushed away. I have not seen him since.

I go about my business these days with firm purpose, but I open each pay envelope with trepidation. One of these times a pink slip of paper will flutter to the floor. Then, sadly enough, it really will be time to say, "Me go now."

Number of Words: 1181 ÷ _____ Minutes Reading Time = Rate _____

I. SEQUENCE

Listed below are some events from the story you just read. Number them from 1 to 6 in the order in which they happened.

_____ **a.** I took a late lunch and bought my fiancée a huge stuffed poodle and a pair of earrings.

_____ **b.** As soon as they departed, I determined not to wait around for the artist any longer.

_____ **c.** I stepped aboard the elevator and said, "Hi. Just getting back from lunch?"

_____ **d.** There I was, putting earrings on a stuffed poodle.

_____ **e.** Glenn Gordon was there to show Mr. Peck artists, so I became one; I drew rectangles furiously.

_____ **f.** It didn't occur to me that he had no idea why I was examining crumpled paper towels in the lavatory.

5 points for each correct answer   SCORE: _____

II. STORY ELEMENTS

Put a check ✓ before the best ending for each sentence.

1. This story would best be described as

_____ **a.** a humorous essay about personnel relationships in a large advertising agency.

_____ **b.** an informative article on how to get along with your boss.

_____ **c.** a first-person description of someone who didn't like his job.

2. The tone and mood of the story are achieved by

_____ **a.** setting a tone of excitement at the very beginning.

_____ **b.** describing the adventures of an employee who wants to get ahead.

_____ **c.** showing how the main character goes from one mishap to another.

3. Although the writer finds himself in ridiculous situations, we are led to believe that he is

_____ **a.** a completely normal victim of circumstances.

_____ **b.** a fool who hasn't got a brain in his head.

_____ **c.** a crafty employee making a fool of his boss.

10 points for correct answer   SCORE: _____

III. CAUSE/EFFECT

Each of the events in column A caused one of the effects in column B. Match each cause with the correct effect.

	A		B
_____ **1.**	The writer was surprised in the art department by his boss and a celebrity.	**a.**	The boss found him examining paper towels in the wastebasket.
_____ **2.**	A secretary whose purse had been stolen asked him to search the men's room.	**b.**	"Me go now," he croaked hoarsely.
_____ **3.**	At the end of the conversation he froze and could think of nothing to say.	**c.**	He began to fasten an earring onto the poodle's ear.
_____ **4.**	He decided to bestow both presents with an original touch.	**d.**	He pretended to be one of the staff artists.

10 points for each correct answer   SCORE: _____

PERFECT TOTAL SCORE: 100   TOTAL SCORE _____

IV. QUESTION FOR THOUGHT

If this story were written from Glenn Gordon's point of view, how might it be different? Give some examples.

The Blizzard
That Blasted the City

Nat Brandt

The deserted streets were clogged with fallen telephone and telegraph poles and blocked by great mountains of snow. Struggling against a fierce, bitterly cold wind, Roscoe Conkling tried to make his way through the streets of New York City.

"It was dark, and it was useless to try to pick out a path, so I went magnificently along shouldering drifts . . . I was pretty well exhausted when I got to Union Square, and, wiping the snow from my eyes, tried to make out the triangles (pathways that crisscrossed the park) there. But it was impossible. There was no light, and I plunged right through on as straight a line as I could determine upon. . . .

"I had got to the middle of the park and was up to my arms in a drift. I pulled the ice and snow from my eyes and held my hands up there till everything was melted off so that I might see; but it was too dark and the snow too blinding. . . ."

It took Conkling 20 minutes to wrestle free from the huge snowdrift, coming "as near giving right up and sinking down there to die as a man can and not do it. Somehow I got out and made my way along." Covered with snow and ice, he finally reached his destination and collapsed inside the lobby. It had taken him three hours to travel two and a half miles (4.1 kilometers). He had fought his way through the worst snowstorm in the history of New York—the Blizzard of 1888.

There have been snowfalls that were greater, hurricanes with winds that were stronger, cold waves when temperatures plummeted lower, but never a combination of the three that was so devastating. The blizzard caught the entire Northeast by surprise and for nearly two days isolated the nation's largest metropolis.

Spring had been in the air as the weekend of March 10–11 began. The winter had been the mildest in 17 years. On Saturday the Barnum, Bailey and Hutchinson Circus had arrived from its winter headquarters and that night staged a torchlight parade through lower Manhattan. Robins were sighted by bird watchers, trees were budding, crocuses were up. Walt Whitman turned in a poem to the *New York Herald,* where he was staff poet; he called it "The First Dandelion" ("Simple and fresh and fair from winter's close emerging . . ./The spring's first dandelion shows its trustful face"). The city's major department stores were planning spring sales. And John J. Meisinger, buyer and manager of Ridley's department store, was the laughingstock of the city. On Friday, March 9, Meisinger had purchased for the "ridiculous low price" of $1,200 a carload of unclaimed snow shovels; a *Herald* reporter happened on the story and called it "Meisinger's Folly." The shovels were delivered to Ridley's on Saturday, the warmest day of the year; temperatures were in the 50's.

Thousands of miles apart two major weather fronts were headed toward the Northeast. The first, a winter snowstorm from the West, had been spawned in the Pacific and was now racing across the continent on freezing winds at the rate of 600 miles (965.4 kilometers) a day. At the same time a warm, moist-air front born in the Gulf of Mexico was moving northward from Georgia.

The outer edges of the two storms converged near Lewes Harbor at the mouth of the Delaware River by Cape Henlopen. The gracefully curved harbor, protected both by its location and a breakwater, was a favored port for coastal vessels.

Hurricane-like winds and blinding snow struck with incredible fury. Anchors broke, rigging and sails were packed with ice and snow, rudders and tillers froze. Vessels ran aground, collided, foundered, while their crews tried desperately to reach safety. Thirty-five of the 50 vessels in the harbor were destroyed.

In New York the rain changed to snow shortly after midnight, the temperature fell rapidly, the wind rose sharply. By six o'clock Monday morning, March 12, as the first city residents were preparing to go to work, the thermometer stood at 23° Fahrenheit (-3° Celsius) and was still falling; winds averaged 36 miles (57.92 kilometers) an hour, with gusts as high as 85 miles (135.1 kilometers) an hour. Driven by the fierce winds, the snow in freakish fashion piled up on one side of some streets, leaving only a slick coating on the other. As the day wore on, the temperature dropped to 5° Fahrenheit (-13° Celsius) and winds climbed to an average of 48 miles (77.3 kilometers) an hour—and no respite was in sight.

What seems amazing is that anyone even contemplated going to work that morning. But in a time before "workers' benefits" and "job security," clerks and laborers were afraid to lose a day's pay. Bankers and stockbrokers were worried about notes and loans due; shopkeepers felt obliged to open their doors for their employees—and besides, most people did not realize the extent of the storm. If they could get out of their homes, they headed for work. For all—rich and poor, young and old—it was a new experience. A blizzard after all, was common enough in the West, but a phenomenon of such proportions

Amazingly many hardy souls did struggle out to work that morning.

had not struck the Northeast before.

"It was as if New York had been a burning candle upon which nature had clapped a snuffer, leaving nothing of the city's activity but a struggling ember," the *New York Evening Sun* declared. ". . . The city's surface was like a wreck-strewn battlefield."

One by one the city's four elevated railroads slowed to a halt, their tracks too slippery with ice to provide traction. One train took 6 hours and

"The city's surface was like a wrecked battlefield."

25 minutes to cover only two blocks. At the height of what was normally the morning rush hour a Third Avenue El train, drawn by a small locomotive called a "dinkie" and pushed by another in back, rammed into a stalled train; an engineer was killed and 14 people injured. Thousands of passengers were stranded high above the streets. Enterprising men ran ladders to the cars and charged the passengers as much as two dollars apiece to climb down.

Streetcar service closed down as the cars ran off their tracks, or the horses could not make any headway. The cars were abandoned where they stood. Walter Hall, a driver on one of the lines, lived for three days in a car.

Commuter service from the suburbs also broke down early. Samuel M. Davis, telegraph operator for the New York Central & Hudson River Railroad at Spuyten Duyvil, just north of Manhattan, was on duty when the 6:40 Croton local reached Duyvil Cut, 150 feet deep (45.72 meters) and 500 feet (152.4 meters) long. The train ran smack into a 30-foot-(9.14 meters) high snowdrift and could not move forward or backward. Two minutes later, the Peekskill local chugged to a halt behind it, then two trains from the West. Within two hours seven trains were strung out behind the Croton local. There were two butcher and grocery shops in town, and Davis "bought everything they had that was eatable—bread, sugar, flour, milk, cured hams, bologna and all the sandwich stuff they had." For the next two days, Davis, his wife and his mother baked bread and made sandwiches and coffee that they lugged up to the passengers aboard the stalled trains.

New York was the focus of the blizzard, but for a radius of 100 miles (160.9 kilometers) around it—at sea, upstate, in New Jersey, Pennsylvania and parts of New England—similar conditions prevailed.

The greatest losses were suffered at sea; nearly 200 ships were wrecked or disappeared. Nine of New York's pilot boats foundered in the harbor or lower bay. Another, the *Starbuck,* cruising off the coast waiting to guide ships into port, her running lights veiled by heavy mist, was hit by the British steamer *Japanese* off Barnegat, New Jersey, when winds of 100 miles (160.9 kilometers) an hour tossed the *Japanese* out of control. Five of the *Starbuck's* crew were lost.

Among the ships that did get through was one carrying immigrants from Lithuania. When a passenger named H. N. Davidsohn emerged into the storm, he assumed that this was the normal climate of the area, and sourly concluded that he might just as well have emigrated to Siberia.

As the day wore on, it became clear that travel in the city itself was next to impossible. The Wall Street Exchange closed down when only 30 members showed up. At the city's 70 banks, only a small fraction of the $63 million in normal daily deposits was received. As a result cashiers refused to certify checks, but, in what was believed an unprecedented action, extended all outstanding loans. Without judges and jury members, the courts closed down. The city prison, the Tombs, was filled to overflowing with men and women who had committed themselves as vagrants; the prison clerk offered to free everyone, but "they all declined with thanks."

Those that did venture out found walking difficult. "There was a fierce cyclonic wind prevailing as we made our way uptown," said Arthur B. Goodkind, who with three friends had decided to head home, "but good cheer and humor kept us going nicely until we reached 86th Street. At this point, one of the wider streets in the then uptown part of the city, we encountered our greatest difficulty. A goodly number of people were standing on the corner, trying to cross over, but the gale-like wind pushed them back at every attempt. A bright idea occurred to someone who had witnessed marching prisoners. He advised that we form in single line, each man with his hands on the shoulders of the man ahead, so that those who crossed successfully might drag the others along. It was in this fashion only that we were able to do what in other conditions would seem to be the absurdly simple business of crossing a city street."

Stores that stocked cold-weather gear sold out quickly. After selling the 45 dozen pairs of gloves he had put aside for the following winter, one Broadway shopkeeper ingeniously cut apart 10 dozen suits of woolen underwear. Each leg was tied with a string at one end and then sold as a pullover cap. The shopkeeper moaned that he had only 10 dozen ear muffs on hand: "They were gone as quickly as snow on a summer's day," he said.

Everywhere, it seemed, strangers were helping each other out. It was not unusual to find people rubbing each other's ears to thaw them out. And the number of rescues was amazing. A World reporter happened to see a young woman fall unconscious into a snowbank; he carried her into a nearby drugstore where she revived. A police officer spied a butcher's cart, its horse collapsing from exhaustion. In the seat was the driver, leaning forward, his head on the dashboard, the reins slipping from his hands. The policeman rubbed the driver's face with snow and with the help of a passerby got him to walk until he was fully conscious. The driver woke up surprised; he thought he had been at home asleep, safe and sound.

Nancy Sankey-Jones remembered seeing a man try for an hour and a half to cross a street. "We watched him start, get one-fourth of the way across and then flung back against the building on the corner. The last time he tried it, he was caught up in a whirl of snow and disappeared from our view."

Hundreds of horses perished, too, as well as enormous numbers of sparrows. Some were eaten by hungry people, for shop supplies dwindled rapidly and the fear of shortages of milk, bread and meat spread throughout the city. Prices for food boomed—eggs going for 40 cents each, the poorest beefsteak for 30 cents a pound, butter for 60 cents.

With outside sources cut off, a shortage of coal also became a widespread fear. Augustus E.

Shoveling out became a gigantic project. Thousands of extra people were hired to help.

Many people ran out of food; so did grocery stores. Prices boomed for what food could be found.

Cron, a 19-year-old messenger for a grocer, recalled how his employer had the good fortune to have 10 tons of coal on hand. Men came from all over, begging for coal, "some men with silk hats on even, and gladly paid as much as a dollar a pailful." Cron made deliveries, too, working until midnight, but four times he had to cut the buttons off the coats he wore because the buttonholes were frozen stiff.

More immediate than the danger of starving or freezing to death was the possibility of uncontrollable fires. With several hundred alarm boxes out of order, fire-department headquarters ordered all engine houses to have four horses ready to hitch to steamers and two to hose carts at all times. In many places, piles of snow insulated hydrants and kept the water lines from freezing, but manuevering through the choked streets was another matter. Answering a summons, one hook-and-ladder company got stuck in a huge snowbank, and even the harnessing of six horses to the wagon failed to budge it.

A major fire did break out in an old four-story building that housed a paper-box factory and was adjacent to tenements inhabited by immigrants. Streams of water pumped at the building froze on contact with the walls and never reached inside. A woman across the street recalled:

"When someone cried fire we looked out and sure enough there it was. The fire engine had an awful time getting around. . . . Ice everywhere, water was taken from the swimming pool. When the firemen got the fire plug working there were rivers of water in rooms, halls, and down the stairs. All the windows on the lane side were broken from the heat and as the men came down from the roof their clothes were solid ice. We weighed their hats at 20 pounds (9.07 kilograms) apiece. We tried to give them hot coffee but had to thaw out the mustaches of those who had them. . . ." By a stroke of fortune, no one was injured in the blaze.

As night approached, the city became wrapped in almost complete darkness. The Metropolitan Telephone Company had asked the electric companies not to start up their dynamos at night because their cables were so entangled with the less-insulated phone wires. "These broken telephone wires would have carried the sparks in all directions into awnings, houses, stores and everywhere else," a spokesman told a *Tribune* reporter, "and the effect would have been terrible." Few gas lamps were working either. Only the lights from the windows of houses and the little red lamps marking fire plugs shed any glow on the snow-clogged streets; the effect was eerie.

All the city's hotels were packed. Doubling and tripling up of strangers was common. At the fashionable Astor House, 200 cots were put in the parlor, halls and even bathrooms—"the last-named apartments," noted the *Herald*,

For those who lived through it, the Blizzard of '88 was an unforgettable experience.

"being quickly taken by the late arrivals . . . even standing room was at a premium in the evening."

Early on Tuesday morning an unusual incident occurred when an immense ice floe from the Hudson River floated back up the bay on the rising tide. The floe slowly headed up the East River, but it was so huge that it got wedged between Brooklyn and Manhattan near the Brooklyn Bridge. The Bridge itself had been closed to pedestrians, and the cable cars that ran back and forth over it were then out of service. Soon hundreds of persons were crossing over the ice field instead. Several tugs appeared and finally the field was broken up, with five men left hugging cakes of ice and drifting out to sea. Three were on a piece as large as Washington Square, two on cakes no larger than a door mat. The tugs rescued all of them.

Gradually, the city struggled back to life. It warmed up a bit as the day progressed—though winds still averaged 45 miles (72.41 kilometers) an hour. The elevated railroads were able to start up on Tuesday, but street traffic continued to be badly bottled up. Getting rid of the snow was the major problem. Shovels were at a premium; Ridley's department store chalked up a neat 50 per cent profit selling all the shovels that John Meisinger had bought for the store. The street-cleaning department hired more than 17,000 extra men at 25 cents an hour to shovel the snow, and tried to rent 1,000 carts from merchants and teamsters.

What amazed even blasé New Yorkers was the good humor that pervaded the city. Signs popped up everywhere on snowbanks: "Keep Off the Grass," "This Bank is closed indefinitely," "It's yours—if you want it," "Don't pick the flowers," "Make us an offer."

Measured in actual inches of snowfall, the blizzard was not impressive—some 16 inches (40.64 centimeters) had fallen on Monday, a little over four more inches (10.16 centimeters) on Tuesday. But other statistics were sobering: nearly 100 persons lost at sea; as many dead in New York or in the region around it; $20 million in property damage in the city alone, and for the people who worked in it, some 700,000 in all, $500,000 lost in wages. And for all of New York's nearly 1.5 million residents it had been an unforgettable experience, almost legendary, one to measure other storms by.

Oddly enough, during the storm New Yorkers kept referring to it as a Dakota blizzard. "It seems to have originated in Dakota, a territory which threatens in our unceremonious nomenclature to be known as the 'Blizzard State,' " a *Herald* editorial declared. "We may do Dakota injustice, which would be unfortunate on the eve of her admission into the family of States, but in the matter of storms she certainly comes off with a bad reputation."

It was meant jokingly, of course, and Dakotans replied in kind. Typical was one of the several telegrams that were addressed to Mayor Hewitt:

"Hurron, Dakota, under a mild spring sun, sends her sympathy to blizzard-stricken New York. If need, you may draw on us for $50 to relieve the storm sufferers."

Roscoe Conkling, whose trek through the city had received wide coverage in the nation's press, also got a telegram, from the office of the Fargo *Argus:*

"The Dakota robins, sitting on orange trees, in blossom, join in thanks for your safe delivery from New York's snowdrifts . . . all join with me in congratulations to you and say: 'Come to the banana belt, where every man is your wellwisher.' "

Number of Words: 3090 ÷ _____ Minutes Reading Time = Rate _____

I. SUMMARY

Below are three statements from the selection. Put a check √ before the one that gives the best summary of the selection.

_____ **1.** The deserted streets were clogged with fallen telephone and telegraph poles and blocked by great mountains of snow.

_____ **2.** A group of survivors known as the Blizzard Men of 1888 continued to observe the anniversary of the storm each year with a dinner at which they swapped anecdotes and rehashed the story of that dreadful day.

_____ **3.** There have been snowfalls that were greater, hurricanes with winds that were stronger, cold waves when temperatures plummeted lower, but never a combination of the three that was so devastating.

15 points for correct answer   SCORE: _____

II. SUPPORTING DETAILS

The first statement below makes a general statement about one aspect of the story. Three of the sentences that follow give details to support this statement, while others do not. Put a check √ before the three details that support the general statement.

Everywhere, it seemed, strangers were helping each other out.

_____ **1.** Those who dared to brave the blizzard wore a strange assortment of clothes.

_____ **2.** Ridley's department store made a neat 50 percent profit selling snow shovels.

_____ **3.** It was not unusual to find people rubbing each other's ears to thaw them out.

_____ **4.** A reporter carried an unconscious woman into a nearby store, where she revived.

_____ **5.** A policeman rubbed the driver's face with snow until he was fully conscious.

15 points for each correct answer   SCORE: _____

III. CAUSE/EFFECT

In each pair of sentences below, one sentence gives a cause; the other gives the effect of that cause. Write C before the sentence that gives the cause and E before the one that tells the effect.

1. _____   Hurricane-like winds and blinding snow struck with incredible fury.

_____   The outer edges of the two storms converged near Lewes Harbor at the mouth of the Delaware River.

2. _____   A Third Avenue El train rammed into a stalled train.

_____   An engineer was killed and 14 people injured.

3. _____   Bank cashiers refused to certify checks.

_____   Only a small fraction of the normal daily deposits was received.

4. _____   Shop supplies dwindled rapidly and fear of shortages spread.

_____   Horses and sparrows were eaten by hungry people.

10 points for each correct answer   SCORE: _____

PERFECT TOTAL SCORE: 100   TOTAL SCORE: _____

IV. QUESTION FOR THOUGHT

If you were to find yourself stranded in a blizzard, what are some of the first steps you would take in order to survive?

Love and the Lie

In 1921 there was a series of baffling thefts in a girls' dormitory at the University of California. Money, jewelry, clothing and other articles were reported missing. School authorities preferred to handle the matter without police assistance, and the girls themselves were assigned to patrol duty. But amateur sleuthing failed, and Margaret Taylor, one of the students, made a formal complaint to the police.

William Wiltberger, a police officer assigned to duty at the college, took charge of the investigation. He toured the secondhand stores and pawnshops in an effort to find the loot, but the thief had been too clever to dispose of it in this obvious manner. He then began to question the 90 girls who lived in the dormitory. He got nowhere. All the girls were from prosperous families, and none seemed to have any reason to steal.

Wiltberger then proposed something altogether new. He had caught the spirit of modern investigation from Police Chief August Vollmer, who was making Berkeley, California, famous as the cradle of scientific crime detection in America. He knew that 23-year-old John A. Larsen, a fellow police officer in Berkeley, had been experimenting with a lie-detecting device that measured a person's respiration, blood pressure and other physical reactions as he or she replied to questions. Now Wiltberger persuaded Larson to set up the apparatus at the college laboratory.

Larson was no ordinary officer of the law. He was a graduate of Boston University and had a Ph.D. from the University of California. He had become interested in criminology while writing a thesis on heredity and fingerprints, which was in line with his studies in biology, physiology and psychiatry. Chief Vollmer had induced him to join the Berkeley Police Department, where he could do special research in police science. That work, however, didn't exempt Larson from pounding a four-to-midnight beat on a regular patrol. Before

Detector

David Redstone

proceeding with the lie tests, young Larson asked the girls to vote their consent. This they unanimously did.

An actual police investigation differs in many ways from those in fiction. In crime fiction the least likely suspect often roams at large through some 200 pages before the detective apprehends the suspect. In real life, when a person finds a body, witnesses a crime or makes a complaint to the police, that person is the first to be examined, so as to eliminate—or incriminate—the least likely suspect. Detectives like to solve mysteries in the shortest possible time, preferably on

page one, so they can go home and soak their feet.

The least likely suspect here was Margaret Taylor, since she was the one who made the complaint. Larson had her take the test first. He did not begin with direct questions such as: "What did you do with Miss So-and-So's handbag?" Subjects mustn't be frightened at the start, for that would influence the graph readings. The girls should be put at ease so that pulse, heartbeat and respi-

ration would be normal when he began their tests.

So, for a while, Larson made casual conversation. Charming conversation it was, too. He and Margaret talked about books, parents, music. He found her intelligent and witty, as well as lovely. She was curious about his work, and soon he found himself talking of his many interests. She told him he was wonderful to be doing so much and to be so ambitious. He almost said she was wonderful too, but caught himself in time. It occurred to him that some criminals and congenital liars have been known to be thoroughly delightful people. Not that this girl. . . .

Then he smiled and said, "Now shall we get down to business?" He adjusted the lie detector and began to read from a list of innocuous questions, later interpolating some like the following:

"Do your parents give you enough money to buy all the things you need at school?"

"Do you enjoy reading crime stories?"

"Do you ever envy your classmates the pretty things they have?"

"Tell me quickly, after each word as you hear it, what you associate with that word or idea: Desk. Tree. Crime. Locket. Rocker. Locker. Purse." She answered easily, without hesitation, and Larson noted the effect on the graph. Key words such as crime, locker, purse had caused no change from the normal in her pulse or breathing. He thanked her gravely and dismissed her.

Several days were spent in making the tests. After they were over, Wiltberger dropped in. "Any results?" he asked.

"Some."

"Any lies?"

"A few."

"Well, lots of people fib a little," Wiltberger remarked. "I suppose you'll have to repeat some of the tests before you make up your mind."

"My mind's made up. But a retest of Margaret Taylor won't do any harm," Larson said. "Will you ask her to come in?"

Wiltberger did so, and left them alone. "There's a special question that I want you to be sure to answer truthfully," said Larson. "It's here on the list. Go ahead, please."

She read it. Her face flushed. Larson watched the blood-pressure indicator. His own face grew warm, because this question was not one he had asked the other subjects. Her answer was a quick "No!" The recording needle jumped with the response. He pointed to the peak on the graph, which showed that she had given an untruthful answer. Confronted with this evidence, she broke down and confessed to the truth. And then she asked *him* the same question.

It was: "Do you love *me?*"

His answer—"I do"—he repeated a year later, at the altar. Which is why he looks back with warm memories to his first lie-detector case.

It was an important case for other reasons. It proved that such a test could be used successfully in a criminal investigation. Larson, by means of the instrument, found the culprit—another of the 90 girls. She confessed when shown that the detector pointed to her guilt. Most of the stolen things, which she had hidden cleverly, were restored to their owners.

Later, Dr. Larson solved a number of important criminal cases that might still be mysteries but for the scientific lie detector, and he taught hundreds of police officers how to use the apparatus. His name came to rank with the top scientists in his field.

Who was proudest to see it there? Margaret Larson, nee Taylor.

Number of Words: 1061 ÷ _____ Minutes Reading Time = Rate _____

I. VOCABULARY

Show that you understand the meaning of the italicized word in each sentence by circling the letter (a, b or c) of the best definition.

1. In fiction, it usually takes a detective much longer to *apprehend* the criminal.
    a. arrest   **b.** understand   **c.** confuse

2. The *innocuous* questions on the list were designed to put the subject at ease.
    a. direct   **b.** insignificant   **c.** serious

3. Later on, more leading questions were *interpolated*.
    a. answered   **b.** mixed in   **c.** explained

4. The subject's physical reactions were measured by the *apparatus*.
    a. equipment   **b.** examiner   **c.** charts

5 points for each correct answer   SCORE: _____

II. SUPPORTING DETAILS

The first sentence below makes a general statement about police officer John A. Larson. Some of the sentences that follow give details to support this statement, while others do not. Put a check √ before the three details that do.

Larson was no ordinary officer of the law.

_____ **1.** He had been experimenting with a new lie-detecting device.

_____ **2.** He was a college graduate with a Ph.D. in criminology.

_____ **3.** He was asked to join the Berkeley Police Department.

_____ **4.** He was doing special research in police science.

_____ **5.** He still pounded a four-to-midnight beat regularly.

10 points for each correct answer   SCORE: _____

III. PROBLEM SOLVING

Five of the following sentences describe the events in solving the mysterious thefts at a girl's school. Put a check √ in front of each of the five steps.

_____ **1.** Money, jewelry and other articles were reported missing.

_____ **2.** Police searched for the loot in secondhand stores.

_____ **3.** They began to question the 90 girls in the dormitory.

_____ **4.** John Larson set up a lie-detecting device at the college.

_____ **5.** Larson fell in love with Margaret Taylor while she was taking the test.

_____ **6.** All the girls were given the lie-detector test.

_____ **7.** The culprit confessed when shown that the detector pointed to her guilt.

10 points for each correct answer   SCORE: _____

PERFECT TOTAL SCORE: 100   TOTAL SCORE: _____

IV. QUESTION FOR THOUGHT

Many courts have declared it illegal to force a person to take a lie-detector test against his or her will. Can you explain why this could be called a violation of one's civil rights?

Call Me A Dancer

Deborah Jowitt

In "Revelations" Judith is unsurpassed, causing audiences to gasp with pleasure.

Midway through Alvin Ailey's "Revelations," she skims onto the stage, face ablaze, wearing a long white ruffled dress, holding up an immense white parasol as if it were a battle flag. It isn't even a starring part, but her vividness, her power, cause the audience to roar with pleasure. Next morning's reviews are likely to speak of the "dance genius of Judith Jamison."

Jamison (pronounced JAM-i-son) is one of the few American-born dancers to compete with glittery international ballet stars for the public's favor. She's also one of the few so-called "modern" dancers to achieve fame without being choreographer-director-star of her own company. On the other hand, she's never been touted as a "star" by the immensely popular Alvin Ailey Dance Theater. The company is full of fine and distinctive dancers to perform works by Ailey as well as by other choreographers. Jamison has her share of good roles, and she shares her good roles with others. "Cry," a long solo Ailey made for her in 1971, is about the closest thing she's had to a vehicle. As Arlene Croce once said in The New Yorker, "Jamison has become a star because people think she ought to be one."

Judith Jamison is 5 feet 10 inches (1.77 meters) tall. Anyone who's seen her on stage is convinced she's 6 feet 5 (1.96 meters). But it's not because of her majestic build and long limbs that your eye goes to her even when she's lined up with the other women in the company, doing the same steps they're doing. Jamison stands out for the subtlety with which she shapes dance movement, for the intensity and lavishness of her performing. She gives the impression of total commitment—that not one jot of her considerable emotional, intellectual or physical power is being withheld from any moment of dancing.

A critic once noted that Jamison can do "comedy or an indecently beautiful arabesque" with equal ease. Not all dancers are versatile; many aren't required to be. They perfect an image of themselves as dancers and continue to display that image with only slight modulations. Given the chance, Jamison can completely change the way she looks and moves. The woman who danced with Mikhail Baryshnikov in Ailey's *pièce d'occasion*, "Pas de Duke"—a woman powerful, challenging and very elegant in a black satin pantsuit—is indeed the same woman who bustles on stage for the last scene in "Revelations," wearing a long, dowdy dress and a floppy-Sunday-go-to-meeting hat. There are such knowing quirks in the way she settles herself on her stool, or wags a rebuking finger at her partner,

Alvin Ailey (left) first saw Judith Jamison in 1965. He has choreographed many of the dances which show off her talent.

or draws her mouth down, or stomps all ungainly into the final dance—you can almost imagine that someone's spry, not-to-be-trifled-with aunt had somehow wandered in among all these dancers and was having the time of her life.

At times, Jamison's dancing looks more African than European-American. Movements that other dancers tend to flatten or make rhythmically square look richly three-dimensional and polyrhythmic when she performs them. Even those beautiful arabesques don't appear studied—she darts out into them; she uncurls her body and they appear. Ailey feels that if Jamison hadn't been a dancer, she might have become an athlete—a runner, perhaps, like Wilma Rudolph— because of her robust physicality, her lust for moving and the naturalness of it. When, at the end of "Cry," the Voices of Harlem belt out, "Right On, Be Free," and Jamison cuts loose— grinning, tossing her head, rippling her long skirt, flailing out with her feet as irrepressibly as an overgrown kid—you under-

stand why other Ailey company women learning "Cry" for the first time are always surprised to discover how difficult the steps are. Jamison doesn't show you steps, she uses them to show you a woman dancing. This ability both to maintain a human dimension and to project superhuman power and radiance is one of her most impressive skills.

Most people cherish her. Her colleagues in the Ailey company volunteer their admiration. "She's practically the only one of us who never skimps," says Peter Woodin. "Even at one of those down matinees in a small city in the middle of nowhere, she doesn't give an inch (2.54 centimeters) under her best." Choreographer Agnes de Mille says, "I think Judy is one of the great dancers of our time. And she's also a remarkable girl, with a first-class, beautiful character."

One of the immediately noticeable nice things about Jamison is that she's scrupulous about acknowledging debts and giving credit where it's due. When she says, "I think . . . I *know* I'm musical," she begins to talk about her family. Her father had a fine voice, played the piano, had hoped at

◀ Among the many stars Judith has danced with is Mikhail (Misha) Baryshnikov (right), a classical ballet dancer who defected from Russia.

one time to study for a concert career. Jamison doesn't know what happened to change his mind and turn him into a sheet-metal worker: "In our family, we don't ask our parents about something personal that happened a long time ago; we wait to be told. Maybe when he's 102, I'll ask him." But Mr. Jamison remained addicted to music. Jamison remembers Saturday afternoons with the whole family (she has an older brother, John, now a long distance bus driver) clustered around the radio, listening to broadcasts from the Metropolitan Opera. And most of the time when she was growing up in Philadelphia, she sang in the young people's choir at Mother Bethel African Methodist Episcopal Church, the first black church in America.

And there were the lessons. Violin, piano, dancing. Judy was tall for her age, loose-limbed, hyperactive. Perhaps Mrs. Jamison feared for her bric-a-brac. She sent her daughter to Marion Cuyjet's Judimar School of Dance, which offered ballet, tap, primitive, you name it. Judy explored them all. What made Cuyjet rare among teachers—Jamison calls her "the golden woman"—was her lack of possessiveness

toward her pupils. She saw to it that Jamison was in the class of every high-powered teacher to do a stint in Philly.

Studying at the Philadelphia Dance Academy, after three misguided semesters—on scholarship—as a psychology major at Fisk, Jamison signed up for a master class given by Agnes de Mille. "Master class," snorts de Mille today. "That's when 'masters' give classes to people who can't manage a fire drill. And then in came this long-limbed beautiful thing—raw, but, oh, brother! . . . And every time I said anything, there was this girl listening, there was this girl watching. So, after a few minutes, I just concentrated on her. It was involuntary. I didn't mean to do it, but finally the class became a private lesson with . . . encumbrances."

Ailey first saw Jamison in the fall of 1965 when she auditioned for a Harry Belafonte television special. The choreographer, Donald McKayle, couldn't use her. Ailey could. At the end of an impromptu speech that Alvin made when Jamison and Royal Ballet premier danseur Anthony Dowell received the 1972 Dance Magazine awards, he said with wonderful vehemence and

Judith Jamison in scene from "Medusa," tames a Grecian gladiator.

In "Caravan," Judith is funny and busy, moving in a new way.

simplicity, "Judy is a lady who came to my company in 1965. A tall, gangly girl with no hair. I always thought she was beautiful."

Jamison, undeniably the antithesis of ballet's romantically pallid, delicately built ideal of a dancer, may not have appreciated Ailey's image of her. Not at first anyway. James Truitte,

one of the original members of the Ailey company, thinks that the first visits the dancers made to Africa, in 1966 and 1967, had an important effect on Jamison. He believes, he says shrewdly, that Judy didn't really *like* herself before then. But in Africa she was clearly a great beauty as well as an outstanding dancer.

Beginning with its 1971 Broadway season, Ailey's company suddenly attracted a new and larger public. And the public and the media accorded Jamison stardom after the premiere of "Cry."

Says Jamison today of the Jamison in 1972, "She was slightly scary. Maybe it was all that publicity—everyone ask-ing me my business. I had this really blown-up idea of what I was. My head didn't get bigger or anything like that. But inside, I was losing track of what I was." She says now, "Don't call me a star. Call me a dancer. That's how I started, and that's all I'm trying to do. Sure it's great to read in the papers, but ...superstar? What's that?...I hope people don't expect me to pop out the stage door wearing a floor-length mink and sweep into a limousine. It's not my style." A minute later she sighs, "Now if I could just become a legend!"

Dancers put in hours of hard daily labor to maintain the requisite bedrock of technical expertise. Unlike most movie stars, they can't get by on attractiveness or charisma. Most remain shrewdly self-appraising. Jamison will say, "I know I'm not a perfect instrument. Things can go wrong no matter how well-prepared I am. Just like in life." She will tell you that any extra poundage lands right on her upper back, making her look matronly. She'll acknowledge, "They tried me in Joyce Trisler's 'Journey'; it's one of my favorites to watch. I think of myself as a lyrical dancer, but don't give me anything too lyrical to do. Give me something halfway in between, and I'll *make* it lyrical. If it's very slow, I get like a brick. I don't consider myself elastic."

There are those who say that Ailey knows Jamison's capabilities better than anyone and shows her off beautifully. There are others who feel that the company's repertory doesn't challenge her enough: "Give her a few arm waves, a toss of the head, a long skirt to throw around; she'll be terrific, but where's the meat in it for her?" It is impossible for Jamison, on stage, to come across as weak. Nevertheless, after 11 years and many ups and downs, it's evident that Jamison trusts and respects Ailey, and he, watching her rehearse "Cry," says with genuine awe, "Every time she does it, it's different—as if she were doing it for the first time."

In many ways, Jamison needs the company as much as the company needs her. Still, like any dancer, she's hungry for challenges. Ailey is good about letting her accept engagements outside the company, and she's beginning to do more of that.

Jamison is eager to be pleased—exhilarated over new roles. In Louis Falco's "Caravan" she's irresistible—funny and busy, throwing her legs around, beckoning the others officiously, doing crazy pratfalls and being tossed around as if she were a bundle of grinning laundry. "Louis gave me a chance to move in a totally, a shockingly different way," and she reveals with pride the fact that the egg-sized lump she got on her arms from doing his falls is now a pea-sized lump. To a dancer, that's progress.

Jamison says, revealingly, that somehow she never thinks of herself as a "career woman." "Only when it comes to paying the rent and the phone bill, do I look on this as a job. To me a career woman is a business executive or a board president. Oh, I'm sure they're having fun too, but their work is more cutthroat than mine."

But knowing what she's gone through, knowing how hard she always tries *not* to worry about her future, one understands completely a remark she once made: "Every dancer lives on the threshold of chucking it."

Number of Words: 1917 ÷ _____ Minutes Reading Time = Rate _____

I. VOCABULARY

Show that you understand the meaning of the italicized word in each sentence by circling the letter (a, b or c) of the best definition.

1. Jamison stands out for the *subtlety* with which she shapes dance movement.
   a. delicacy   **b.** strength   **c.** beauty

2. Jamison is the *antithesis* of ballet's romantically pallid, delicately built ideal of a dancer.
   a. equal   **b.** modern version   **c.** direct opposite

3. One of the immediately noticeable things about Jamison is that she's *scrupulous* about acknowledging debts.
   a. difficult   **b.** honest   **c.** aware

4. Jamison is eager to be pleased—*exhilarated* over new roles.
   a. stimulated   **b.** terrified   **c.** displeased

5 points for each correct answer   SCORE: _____

II. FACT/OPINION

Write F before each sentence that states a fact. Write O before each sentence that states an opinion.

_____ 1. Ailey first saw Jamison in the fall of 1965 when she auditioned for a television special.

_____ 2. Unlike movie stars, most dancers remain shrewdly self-appraising.

_____ 3. In many ways, Jamison needs the company as much as the company needs her.

_____ 4. Every dancer lives on the threshold of chucking it.

10 points for each correct answer   SCORE: _____

III. OUTLINING

Complete the following outline by writing the correct answer (a, b, c or d) in its proper place.

  a. She is more versatile than most dancers.
  b. She shares her good roles with others.
  c. She is too tall and powerful for some roles.
  d. She stands out from other dancers even when doing the same steps.
  e. She gives the impression of total commitment.

  I. Judith Jamison has achieved unique stardom as a dancer.
    A. She's never been touted as a star by her company.
      1. The company is full of fine dancers.
      2. _____
    B. _____
      1. She shapes each movement with great subtlety.
      2. She performs with intensity and lavishness.
      3. _____
 II. _____
    A. She can easily change the way she looks and moves.
    B. She can do comedy or arabesque with equal ease.
III. She has definite shortcomings.
    A. She can't do anything too liquid.
    B. She doesn't consider herself elastic.
    C. Not all roles are suitable for her.
      1. _____
      2. Her biggest success was in a role created for her.

8 points for each correct answer   SCORE: _____

PERFECT TOTAL SCORE: 100   TOTAL SCORE: _____

IV. QUESTION FOR THOUGHT

Why does a professional dancer always feel a certain amount of insecurity about his or her future?

ON THE ROAD:

A Family Affair

Sam Moses

On most Wednesday evenings after supper, Lester and Ivadene Claycomb climb into their 34,000-pound (15,422-kilogram), $52,000 Kenworth diesel rig and begin the long haul from their home in Duncansville, Pennsylvania, to Homestead, Florida. Stopping only for meals, coffee and a few hours sleep in the bunk of the cab, they arrive Friday morning. After the trailer is unloaded, they drive across town to pick up a load of produce—watermelons, crates of lettuce, sacks of potatoes—and head home again, arriving Saturday night after a round trip of over 2500 miles (4022.5 kilometers).

Monday morning, often as early as six o'clock, Lester hastens across the lawn to the spacious garage behind their house where, alone, he continues the eternal chore of maintaining the couple's four diesel rigs. Ivadene, meanwhile, attacks the laundry and household chores and in the afternoon

attends to the company's business; scheduling trips, dickering with freight dispatchers, paying bills, keeping the books. On many Tuesday afternoons they make a 300-mile (482.7-kilometer) round trip in the Kenworth to York, Pennsylvania, to deliver local produce, returning home just before dawn. And on Wednesday nights they usually leave for Florida again.

Lester Claycomb is 73 years old; Ivadene is 67. They have been married 51 years and have worked together in the interstate trucking business for 46 of those years. Their story is not one of two downtrodden oldsters forced by the system to work their fingers to the bone, but of two vital, energetic, useful people who love their work—and each other.

They appear to be opposites: Ivadene is taller than Lester and 10 pounds (4.5 kilograms) heavier, a gabber who loves an audience, while Lester is so laconic that he sometimes seems mute. But these differences are superficial; in their hearts, where it counts, they are very similar.

It is a Wednesday evening in January and Lester and Ivadene are enroute to Florida. There is a feeling of relief in the rig, a tacit sigh in the air. There is always that aura at the commencement of a trip; they labor so hard at home that their initial hours in the truck are actually relaxing. The cab is their cocoon.

A light snow falls softly as they head for Interstate 70. The windshield wipers flap like a metronome; amber lights glow on the instrument panel, warming the atmosphere in the cab. There's a CB radio, but it is difficult to imagine Lester talking into it. "Aw, it just makes noise," he says. And that is about all Lester will say for the next few hours.

The road is a place where Ivadene is silent as well. "If Lester talks to me, I answer him," she says. "But I don't bother him. We can ride for 100 miles (160.9 kilometers) without saying a word. I'm watching the road all the time, though. When the old man starts getting heavy-eyed, weaving around the road about two in the morning, I say, 'Okay, it's time to pull over.'"

The bunk above and behind the seats in the cab is dark and cozy and big enough for two. "We crawl around there like two-year olds," says Ivadene. In the bunk are two goose-down sleeping bags and two foam pillows.

Lester and Ivadene began dating when he was 21 and she was 15. Says Ivadene, "Lester was the jokester type; even when he was telling the truth he had a grin on him. My daddy didn't know how to take him."

A year later, in February, 1928, they were married, and four years hence their first offspring—Althea—was born. That same year Lester and Ivadene ventured into the trucking business.

They started with one truck, the bed of which they built themselves: Lester hammered and Ivadene held. The truck was longer than their garage, so they ignored the snow that blustered through the open door while they worked, attired in extra coveralls. After a driver Lester had employed for a short haul wrecked the truck, they rebuilt it and traded it for a semi.

Over the next two decades, six more youngsters were born to Ivadene and Lester. On many trips Ivadene took at least one of her children along; other times she stayed home and Lester took one of the children himself. The fondest childhood memories of daughter Judy, now 31, are the days she spent traveling with her father, standing up in the seat

next to him as he drove along, high above the other cars on the highway, her arm around his shoulder.

At its peak, in 1948, the Claycombs' business included 14 trucks and 19 trailers, and they employed 14 drivers. "We've seen some rough times, had a lot of hard luck and heartaches. After 47 years I sometimes get tired and wish we didn't live such a life. But we've never known anything but trucks. We wouldn't know what to do with ourselves if we quit.

"I'm always available if the old man needs help in the garage," she continues. "I'm right down there with him under the truck. Last trip from Florida we unloaded a full load of products in two hours flat. Lester told me to take it a little easy, and I said, 'You're a good one to talk, because you ain't stoppin' either!' He hasn't taken a day off in 47 years."

A lifetime of hard labor can be read in Lester's hands. Emerging from forearms as muscular as a weight lifters, the hands are impressively strong from thousands of hours of twisting wrenches, shifting the multiple gears on his trucks and wrestling with an enormous steering wheel. The fin-

gers are so broad there appears to be almost no space between them, with knuckles hard like stones; they look too clubby to manage a shirt button, but these are the same fingers that have gently changed the diapers of an infant daughter in the bunk of a rig at some rest spot along the highway.

"I can't do without Pap," says Ivadene. "I can take care of business, but I got to have a good mechanic." The statement clearly applies to their life as well as their work. Lester understands trucks, Ivadene understands people. He trusts her and isn't threatened by a woman doing what she can do better than he. She, in return, is unfailingly supportive.

"We've had ups and downs," says Ivadene. "But we've toughed it out. Cooperation: that's what it takes. You got to give and take. Be honest and learn to agree. Marriage can be a wonderful thing if two people understand each other."

"They don't realize how happy they are working together," says daughter Judy. "They don't have a lot of money, but if they did they wouldn't even know it. My mother really loves that man; my father could go out and dig ditches, and she would be right with him. I would like to end my own life with that kind of bond."

"It's nice to have a partner, is what it is," says Ivadene.

Number of Words: 1177 ÷ _____ Minutes Reading Time = Rate _____

I. MAIN IDEA

In each group of sentences below, one sentence gives a main idea and the other two illustrate or support it. Circle the letter (a, b or c) of the sentence that states the main idea in each group.

1. **a.** She's a talker who loves an audience, while he is so laconic that he sometimes seems mute.
    b. They appear to be opposites, but these differences are superficial.
    c. Ivadene is taller than Lester and 10 pounds heavier.

2. **a.** There is a feeling of relief in the rig, a tacit sigh in the air.
    b. They labor so hard at home that their initial hours in the truck are actually relaxing.
    c. The cab is their cocoon.

3. **a.** A lifetime of hard work can be read in Lester's hands.
    b. The hands are impressively strong from thousands of hours of twisting wrenches and shifting gears.
    c. The fingers are broad and the knuckles hard like stones.

10 points for each correct answer   SCORE: _____

II. SUMMARY

Below are three statements from the selection. Put a check √ before the one that gives the best summary of the selection.

_____ **1.** Lester hasn't taken a day off in 47 years.

_____ **2.** Their story is that of two vital, energetic, useful people who love their work—and each other.

_____ **3.** "We wouldn't know what to do with ourselves if we quit."

20 points for correct answer   SCORE: _____

III. SKIMMING

Skim through the selection to find the answer to each of the following questions. Write the answers in the blanks.

1. How long have the Claycombs been married? _____
2. In what business are the Claycombs engaged? _____
3. In what year did their business reach its peak? _____
4. What is their destination when they begin their weekly journey on Wednesday evening? _____

5 points for each correct answer   SCORE: _____

IV. GENERALIZATIONS

Certain generalizations may be made based on the information in this story. Put a check √ before each of the three sentences that makes a valid generalization.

_____ **1.** Long-distance trucking is a demoralizing occupation.

_____ **2.** People do not lose their usefulness just because they have reached a certain age.

_____ **3.** A lifetime of hard work and cooperation can be better for a marriage than material wealth.

_____ **4.** Children raised "on the road" are usually unhappy.

_____ **5.** Nonverbal communication is an important element of a good marriage.

10 points for each correct answer   SCORE: _____

PERFECT TOTAL SCORE: 100   TOTAL SCORE: _____

V. QUESTIONS FOR THOUGHT

Do you think the Claycombs would give up their exhausting way of life if they could afford to? Why or why not?

Barry Manilow:

The Making of a Superstar

Robert Spitz

I grew up on Division Street in Brooklyn, slums and danger being the best words to describe it. Roots are really an incredible thing, especially when you've been able to pull yourself out of an awful situation and can look back on it fondly. I mean, I wouldn't have traded it for the suburbs any day. It was New York, it was exciting and you never knew what was going to happen next. I may be a slum kid by definition, but I lived in a very nice house and was treated terrifically by my parents and grandparents, and I never knew, at the time, I was a slum kid.

But my father got tired of it early. He took off when I was two and left us there to fend for ourselves. It was rough being a skinny kid on the streets.

I came from a musical household, heavy on the pop stuff of the day. We had an old record player which continuously played the Andrew Sisters and all the big band music. But my greatest musical incentive was when I got Willie Murphy as a gift for my bar mitzvah. He became my stepfather, and he drove a truck and was a jazz nut. He took me to my first jazz concert—Gerry Mulligan at Town Hall. I didn't know that kind of music existed. Willie also threw out my accordion and got me a piano and started turning me on to Ted Heath and Chris Connor and shows like The King and I and Carousel and The Most Happy Fella. That really got me into music on my own.

I got through high school pretty easily, but, when I got out, I had no idea what I wanted to do. Music as a profession never crossed my mind. Nobody I knew considered it at the time. It was just a hobby.

I enrolled in an advertising course at City College nights and clipped ads in an ad agency during the day. That got to me quick, and I switched to the

New York College of Music and, then, Julliard, and I worked in the mailroom at CBS to get by.

At the time, I never really paid attention to rock or commercial radio. I was into jazz. But the first time pop/rock music really knocked me out was when I heard the Beatles. And it wasn't really the Beatles that knocked me out—it was what was happening behind them. It was the arrangements and the production, because it was the first time (with rock music) that I heard somebody back there thinking about what they were doing. It wasn't just four guys getting up and making music. Somebody else had put it together. And I said, "That's what I want to be when I grow up." I wasn't in the music business yet, per se. But I now knew what I wanted to do.

I knocked around at CBS for about eight years doing various assignments. I was a musical director of an amateur series they had called *Callback,* which won a number of awards, and I did a number of Ed Sullivan TV specials.

I met Bette Midler in the spring of 1972. I wasn't really impressed with her all that much during rehearsal. She kind of walked through it. But that night—well, it was as if she was lip-synching, because she knocked me out. I mean, to hear Bette for the first time is a surprise to anyone with any musical taste. She was marvelous. I knew she was going to be a big, big singer once a few more people got to hear her. After the show, I walked backstage and said, "Hey kid, where did this incredible voice of yours come from?" And, as they say in the movies, that was the start of a beautiful relationship.

I became Bette's arranger, conductor and pianist, and her career just took off. We had the time of our lives.

I also became her producer and album arranger, and we worked on the act a lot.

My being with Bette—I don't know if it made me a more successful musician, but it gave me a better idea of how to put on an interesting, lively show and make a better record.

I can communicate what I want very easily to other musicians; I play the piano exactly to what I want to hear. It used to take Bette a long time to communicate to me what she wanted to hear and what she wanted the song to sound like; that's because she doesn't play an instrument. She'd say to me, "Make it purple." Purple—what does that mean?—slow, or fast or what? Nonmusicians take longer to communicate their music and express themselves musically, even though their music may be brilliant.

I loved being in the studio with Bette. It was a unique experience, and I felt as though it was the pediatric ward in a hospital, where something special was created and preserved. It's a totally artistic environment, and people are generally happy when recording.

It was during the time we were working on the first album, *The Devine Miss M.*, that I was introduced to Larry Uttal and Irv Biegel, the president and vice-president of a record company. They had heard some of the music that I had written and sung, and suggested that I give it a try on my own. They would be glad to have me as one of their artists. Well, this was a big decision, but it was something that I had always dreamed of doing, and I was not about to pass up the chance. So I signed a contract with them.

But they said, "You cannot make an album for us unless you go out on the road with it and perform the music." From a record company's point of view, this is the only way of promoting their interests. A record album costs on the average of $35,000 to $100,000 to produce, and nobody will know that it's there after it's finished unless the artist performs it in public. It's not like ten years ago when record prices were much lower and consumers might speculate and pick up an album because of word-of-mouth or because they liked the cover.

So I said, "Okay." And I worked out a deal with Bette so I could perform a few numbers right in the middle of her act and I could still continue to be her conductor.

The first gig I did my numbers with Bette was in front of 8,000 people in Columbia, Maryland, after she had driven them absolutely crazy with the first half of her show. I was sitting at the piano conducting "Do You Wanna Dance?" and I knew, as I finished the last note, with people screaming and yelling as Bette went off, that after the intermission the first one they were going to see was me. I wasn't on the bill. I was just listed on the program as musical director. So nobody knew that I was going to come out and sing three of my original numbers in the middle of this bedlam. It was outdoors, and you could not see the end of the heads. So what did I do? What any other red-blooded American boy would do—*I threw up!* Really!

But the worst part was toward the end of the tour. We were playing New York City—home. And I practically knew everybody in the audience. All my friends. And this colossal theater. Judy Garland played there—all the greats. And so, one night I found myself singing on the stage of the Palace Theatre. It was an awesome experience for me. And my career took off from there. It's been like a dream ever since.

I don't specialize in lyrics— I'm a musician, and the music comes very easy to me—lyrics don't, and I know that. Sometimes I come up with something that, at least, makes sense and I'm not too embarrassed about, but most of the time, I'm totally moronic when I write my own lyrics. And I will call somebody and say, "Listen, I've got this terrific idea; will you please put it down right?"

I like to write by myself; I don't think there are many established collaborators who can work in tandem in the same room. It's too personal a thing, and it's inhibitive. I make a million mistakes musically and vocally when I try to compose,

and it's just something I have to go through by myself.

It's difficult to find the right people to work for you. My attorney became my manager, and I was just lucky. I had worked with Miles Lourie, my attorney, for five years, and he handled all my legal matters. So it was natural for him to become my manager. I kept asking him, "What do I do now? How do I do this?" And I continuously asked him for advice that really didn't pertain to law anymore. And he said, "Barry, I think it's time we got married." When you get a manager, you couldn't be more married.

I don't know how you'd really peg my style. I hated the term "M-O-R" (middle-of-the-road) in the beginning because M-O-R, for all these years, all the years I had grown up, typified all the music I *didn't* want to be associated with. When the reviews came back saying, "M-O-R," saying "easy listening," saying, "pop," I kept cringing and saying, "No! That's not it!" My music had a sound different from Andy Williams or Vicki Carr. It has more of a street sound, more of a city sound.

Well, I'm still doing the same music, and they still call it M-O-R, but there are other people who are joining me, and I'm not embarrassed anymore. In fact, I think my audience has grown because of the label. A lot of older people with an aversion to listening to anything called rock will listen to me and enjoy what I'm doing. I think of what I do first as making music, but I also think of myself as a rock singer.

I know that if I just went out on the stage and sang for an hour and a half, I'd be boring. That's why we worked so hard on putting some kind of show together before we began our first tour. Other performers get caught up in their acclaim and forget that they have to keep up the interest during their performance. Singing straight is just not enough anymore—not for eight or ten bucks a ticket. You have to be good! Getting up there and being able to talk to your audience throughout your performance is a serious part of putting on a concert. My forte is, of course, making music, but I had to force myself to learn how to get up there and talk a little, not sounding too slick. I'm always on edge doing that because I have to know exactly what to say. I'm no

"I just have to give my best, and then a little more."

good as an ad-libber. I want the audience to get to know me; I want them to get to know the band. I think that if they get to know me—whether they are into the music or not—the music will mean more to them.

For me every performance is life or death. And every time I walk onto the stage, it's critical. I just have to give my best, and then a little more.

Number of Words: 1942 ÷ _____ Minutes Reading Time = Rate _____

I. CRITICAL THINKING

Circle the letter of the best answer to each question.

1. Why was Barry Manilow so impressed by the Beatles' music?
   a. He felt that they had found the secret of making a fortune in the world of pop music.
   b. He appreciated the fact that there was intelligent thought behind their music.
   c. He knew that they were slum kids, like himself, who had "made good."

2. Why is Manilow concerned about putting quality material on his records?
   a. He knows that most record buyers have tastes similar to his own.
   b. He knows that good songs will "sell themselves" and make it unnecessary for him to make personal appearances.
   c. He realizes that records are expensive and feels that his fans deserve their money's worth.

3. Why does Manilow refer to having a manager as "being married?"
   a. The manager gets an equal share of the star's earnings.
   b. The manager is closely involved with every aspect of the star's career.
   c. The star spends all of his or her working time with the manager.

4. Why did he at first dislike the term "middle-of-the-road" as a description of his music?
   a. It sounded as though he had no real style of his own.
   b. It sounded like the kind of street music he was trying to get away from.
   c. He felt that only old people listened to that type of music.

10 points for each correct answer   SCORE: _____

II. CHARACTERIZATION

Put a check ✓ before five characteristics that you believe Barry Manilow possesses, based on information in the story.

_____ **a.** ashamed of his background

_____ **b.** well-educated

_____ **c.** serious about music

_____ **d.** high-strung and temperamental

_____ **e.** respects talents of others

_____ **f.** appreciates his fans

_____ **g.** selfish

_____ **h.** mainly concerned with money

_____ **i.** honest about his shortcomings

_____ **j.** makes rash decisions

6 points for each correct answer   SCORE: _____

III. SKIMMING

Skim through the selection to find the answer to each of the following questions. Write the answers in the blanks.

1. Which two music schools did Manilow attend? _____
   _____

2. What was his connection with the amateur series "Callback"? _____

3. What is the cost of producing a record album? _____

4. Where did Manilow first perform his own numbers in public? _____

5. Who is Miles Lourie?_____

6 points for each correct answer   SCORE: _____

PERFECT TOTAL SCORE: 100   TOTAL SCORE: _____

IV. QUESTION FOR THOUGHT

What characteristics, if any, set Barry Manilow apart from most other pop or rock singers? Explain your answer.

Brand New Day

George and Helen Papashvily

At five o'clock in the morning the engines stopped, and after 37 days the boat was quiet.

We were in America.

I got up, stepped over the other men and looked out the porthole. Water and fog. We were anchoring off an island. I dressed and went on deck.

Then my troubles began. What to do? This was a Greek boat and I was in steerage, so by the time we were halfway out I had spent all my landing money for extra food.

Hassan, the Turk, one of the six who slept in the cabin with me, came up the ladder.

"I told you so," he said as soon as he saw me. "Now we are in America and you have no money to land. They send you home. No money, no going ashore. What a disgrace."

Hassan had been satisfied to starve on black olives and salt cheese all the way from Gibraltar, and he begrudged every skewer of lamb I bribed away from the first-cabin steward.

We went down the gangplank into the big room. Passengers with pictures in their hands were rushing frantically around to match them to a relative. Before their tables the inspectors were occupied with long lines of people.

The visitors' door opened and a fellow with a big pile of striped blue-and-white cotton caps with visors and a top button came in. He went first to an old man near the window, then to a Cossack in the line. At last he came to me.

"Look," he said in Russian, "look at your hat. You want to be a greenhorn all your life? Do you expect to see anybody in the U.S.A. still with a fur hat? The customs inspector, the doctor, the captain—are they wearing fur hats? Certainly not."

I didn't say anything.

"Look," he said, "I'm sorry for you. I was a greenhorn once myself. I wouldn't want to see anybody make my mistakes. Look, I have caps. See, from such rich striped material. Like wears railroad engineers, and house painters and coal miners." He spun one around on his finger. "Don't be afraid. It's a cap in real American style. With this cap on your head, they couldn't tell you from a citizen. I'm positively guaranteeing. And I'm trading you this cap even for your old fur hat. Trading even. You don't have to give me one penny."

Now it is true that I had bought my fur hat new for the trip. It was a fine skin, a silver lamb, and in Russia it would have lasted me a lifetime. Still—

"I'll tell you," the cap man said. "So you can remember all your life you made money the first hour you were in America, I give you a cap and a dollar besides. Done?"

I took off my own hat and put on his cap. It was small and sat well up on my head, but then in America one dresses like an American, and it is a satisfaction always to be in the best style. So I got my first dollar.

Ysaacs, a Syrian, lounged on the bench and watched all through the bargain. He was from our cabin, too, and he knew I was worried about the money to show the examiners. But now, as soon as the cap man went on to the next customer, Ysaacs explained a way to facilitate getting by the examiners—a good way.

Such a very good way, in fact, that when the inspector examined my passport and entry permit I was ready.

"Do you have friends meeting you?" he queried me. "Do you have money to support yourself?"

I withdrew a round fat roll of green American money—tens, twenties—a nice thick pile encircled with a rubber band.

"O.K.," he said. "Proceed." He stamped my papers.

I secured my baggage and took the money roll back again to Ysaacs' friend, the money lender, so he could rent it over again to another man. One dollar was all he charged to use it for each landing. Really a bargain.

On the outer platform, I met Zurabeg, who had been down in steerage, too. But Zurabeg was no greenhorn coming for the first time. Zurabeg was an American citizen with papers to prove it, and a friend of Buffalo Bill besides. This Zurabeg came first to America 20 years before as a trick-show rider, and later he was boss cook on

the road with Buffalo Bill. Every few years, Zurabeg, whenever he saved enough money, went home to find a wife—but so far with no luck.

"Can't land?" he asked me.

"No, I can land," I said, "but I have no money to pay the little boat to carry me to shore." A small boat went chugging back and forth taking off the discharged passengers. "I try to make up my mind to swim, but if I swim how will I carry my baggage? It would need two trips at least."

"Listen, donkey-head," Zurabeg said, "this is America. The carrying boat is free. It belongs to my government. They take us for nothing. Come on."

So we got to the shore.

And there—the streets, the people, the noise. The faces flashing by—and by again. The screams and chatter and cries. But most of all the motion, back and forth, back and forth, pressing deeper and deeper on my eyeballs.

We walked a few blocks before I remembered my landing cards, passport and visas. I took them out and tore them into little pieces and threw them in an ash can. "They can't prove I'm not a citizen, now," I said. "What we do next?"

"We get jobs," Zurabeg told me. "I show you."

We went to an employment agency. Conveniently, the man spoke Russian. He gave Zurabeg a ticket right away to start in a Russian restaurant as first cook.

"Now, your friend? What can you do?" he asked me.

"I am a worker in decorative leather, particularly specializing in the ornamenting of crop handles according to the traditional designs," I said.

"This is the U.S.A.," the employment agent said. "No horses; we have automobiles and other vehicles. What else can you do?"

Fortunately my father was a man of immense foresight, and I have two trades. His contention was that in the days when a man starves with one, by the other he may eat.

I said, "I am also a swordmaker—short blades or long; daggers with or without chasing; hunting knives, plain or ornamental; tempering, fitting, pointing. . . ."

"A crop maker—a sword pointer. You better take him along for a dishwasher," he said to Zurabeg. "They can always use another dishwasher."

We went down into the earth and flew through tunnels in a

train. It was like caves where giant bats sleep, and it smelled even worse.

The restaurant was on a side street and the lady owner spoke kindly. "I remember you from the tearoom," she said to Zurabeg. "I congratulate myself on getting you."

Zurabeg spoke grandly: "My friend—," he waved toward me—"will be a dishwasher."

I made a bow.

The kitchen was small and hot and fat—like inside of a pig's stomach. Zurabeg unpacked his knives, put on his cap and, at home at once, started to dice celery.

"You can wash these," the owner said to me. "At four we have a party."

It was a trayful of glasses. And such glasses—thin bubbles, set on stems, that would hardly hold a sip. The first one snapped in my hand, the second dissolved, the third to tenth I got washed, the eleventh was already cracked, the twelfth rang once on the pan edge and was silent.

I might be there yet, but just as I carried the first trayful to the service slot, the restaurant cat ran between my feet.

When I got all the glass swept up, I told Zurabeg, "Now, we have to eat. It's noon. I watch the customers eat. It makes me hungry. Prepare a shashlik and some cucumbers, and we enjoy our first meal for good luck in the New World."

"This is a restaurant," Zurabeg said. "We get to eat when the customers go, and you get what the customers leave. Try again with the glasses and remember my reputation. Please."

I found a quart of sour cream and went into the back alley and ate that and some bread and a jar of caviar that was very salty—packed for export, no doubt.

The restaurant owner found me. I stood up. "Please," she said, "please go on. Eat sour cream. But after, could you go away? Far away? With no hard feelings. The glasses—the caviar—it's expensive for me—and at the same time I don't want to make your friend mad. I need a good cook. If you could just go away? Quietly? Just disappear, so to speak? I give you five dollars."

"I didn't do anything," I said, "so you don't have to pay me. All in all, a restaurant probably isn't my fate. You can tell Zurabeg afterward."

She brought my cap and a paper bag. I went down through the alley and into the street. I walked. I walked until my feet took fire in my shoes and my neck ached from looking. I walked for hours. I couldn't even be sure it was the same day. I tried some English on a few men that passed. "What watch?" I said. But they pushed by me so I knew I had it wrong. I tried another man. "How many clock?" He showed me on his wrist. Four-thirty.

A wonderful place. Rapidly, if one applies oneself, one speaks the English.

I came to a park and went in and found a place under a tree and took off my shoes and lay down. I looked in the bag the restaurant owner gave me. A sandwich of bologna and a nickel—to begin in America with.

What to do? While I decided, I slept.

A policeman was waking me up. He spoke. I shook my head I can't understand. Then with hands, with legs, rolling his eyes, turning his head, with motions, with gestures, he showed me to lie on the grass is forbidden. But one is welcome to the seats instead. All free seats in this park. No charge for anybody. What a country.

But I was puzzled. There were iron armrests every two feet along the benches. How could I distribute myself under them? I tried one leg. Then the other. But when I was under how could I turn around? Then, whatever way I did it, my chin was always caught by the hoop. While I thought this over, I walked and bought peanuts with my nickel and fed the squirrels.

Lights began to come on in the towers around the park. It was almost dark. I found a sandy patch under a rock on little bluff above the drive. I cut a stick and built a fire of twigs and broiled my bologna over it and ate the bread. It lasted very short. Then I rolled up my cap for a pillow and went to sleep.

I was tired from America, and I slept some hours. It must have been almost midnight when the light flashed in my face. I sat up. It was from the head lamp of a touring car choking along on the road below me. While I watched, the engine coughed and died. A man got out. For more than an hour he knocked with tools and opened the hood and closed it again.

Then I slid down the bank. I showed him with my hands and feet and head, like the policeman: "Give me the tools and let me try." He handed them over and sat down on the bench.

I checked the spark plugs and the distributor, the timer and the coils. I inspected the feed line, the ignition, the gas gauge. In between I cranked, until I cranked my heart out onto the ground. Still the car wouldn't budge.

I got mad and then furious and then I kicked the radiator as hard as I could. The car was an old Model T, and it started with a snort that shook the chassis like an aspen.

The man came running up. He was laughing and he shook my hands and talked at me and asked questions. But the policeman's method didn't work. Signs weren't enough. I remembered my dictionary—English-Russian, Russian-English—it went both ways. I took it from my pocket and showed the man. Holding it under the headlights, he thumbed through.

"Work?" he found.

I looked at the Russian word beside it and shook my head.

"Home?" he turned to that.

"No," again.

I took the dictionary. "Boat. Today."

"Come home"—he showed me the words—"with me—" he pointed to himself. "Eat. Sleep. Job," he said. "Job. Tomorrow."

"Automobiles?" I said. We have the same word in the Georgian language.

"Automobiles." He was pleased we found one word together.

We got in his car, and he took me through miles and miles of streets with houses on both sides of every one of them until we came to his own. We went in and we ate and we drank and ate and drank again. For that, fortunately, you need no words.

Then his wife showed me a room, and I went to bed. As I fell asleep, I thought to myself: Well, now, I have lived one whole day in America and just like they say—America is a country where anything, anything at all can happen.

And in 20 years—about this I never changed my mind.

Number of Words: 2305 ÷ _____ Minutes Reading Time = Rate _____

I. GENERALIZATIONS

Certain generalizations may be made based on the information in this story. Put a check ✓ before three of the sentences that make a valid generalization.

_____ **1.** People often took advantage of immigrants from the moment they landed.

_____ **2.** Many immigrants were eager to become "Americanized" as soon as possible.

_____ **3.** Some immigrants had been trained in skills that were useless in America.

_____ **4.** A large percentage of immigrants got good jobs almost as soon as they arrived.

_____ **5.** Most immigrants found that America looked very much the same as their homeland.

10 points for each correct answer   SCORE: _____

II. CRITICAL THINKING

Circle the letter of the best answer to each question.

1. Why were immigrants required to prove that they had American money?
   a. American money was better than foreign money.
   b. The inspectors were working illegally with the moneylenders.
   c. The government wanted to be sure that the immigrants would not be a burden to others.
2. Why were some highly skilled workers forced to take menial jobs?
   a. There was no demand for their skills in America.
   b. There were too many of them arriving at once.
   c. Many Americans were skilled in the same trades as the arriving immigrants.

3. Why did the writer use his only nickel to buy peanuts for the squirrels?
    a. He did not understand the value of American money.
    b. He cared more about animals than he did for himself.
    c. He was an optimist and not worried about the future.

10 points for each correct answer   SCORE: _____

III. SKIMMING

Skim through the story to find the answer to each question. Circle the letter of the right answer.

1. How long did the ocean crossing take?
    a. 22 days   **b.** 29 days   **c.** 37 days
2. Which of these passengers came from Syria?
    a. Hassan   **b.** Ysaacs   **c.** Zurabeg
3. How much did the restaurant owner offer to pay the writer to go away?
    a. five dollars   **b.** a nickel   **c.** fifty dollars
4. Which of these was not one of the author's trades in Russia?
    a. swordmaker   **b.** furrier   **c.** crop maker

10 points for each correct answer   SCORE: _____

PERFECT TOTAL SCORE: 100   TOTAL SCORE: _____

IV. QUESTION FOR THOUGHT

Do you think the writer would have fared better in America if he had spoken the language and possessed different skills? Give reasons for your answer.

They Call It "Orienteering"

Mark Wexler

Talk about feeling like a fool. There I was, a compass in one hand, a map in the other and up to my knees in a slimy bog. Standing a few feet away, two cute little blonde girls stared down at me. "Hey, mister," one of them jeered. "What'ya doing in there? You won't find a control flag in the middle of that muck." I had to laugh. "I guess I'm lost," I said.

There really was no guesswork about it. I was as lost as I've ever been in my life. But it soon proved to be only the first of many confused moments for me that day. I was trying to outmaneuver some 300 other weekend nature lovers through dense forest in central Michigan. We were all competing in an exercise known as "orienteering" and I had just committed a cardinal sin. Specifically, I had tried to get from one checkpoint to another by way of a straight line, without first carefully studying my map.

Knowing how to read a map is what orienteering—a woodsy version of the old treasure hunt game—is all about. Although it is still a relatively obscure pastime, the number of people addicted to it in some parts of the country has quadrupled and it is not hard to figure out why. As I discovered for myself in Michigan, orienteering is perfect for today's suburban conservationist. It is more than a mere trek in the woods but less than an all-out battle for sur-

Getting lost is part of the learning process for newcomers to orienteering.

vival. And it is a competitive sport for young and old, male and female, of which it can honestly be said that winning matters less than running the course well.

Originally, orienteering was conceived by a Swedish youth leader who toughened up a cross-country race for youngsters by laying a course through the woods and throwing in some compasses and topographic maps. That was in 1918. Today, orienteering is compulsory in Swedish public schools and some 16,000 contestants from two dozen countries meet in Stockholm each summer to compete in the largest single competitive sporting event in the world—the O-rin-

gen. In Japan, the sport is so popular that orienteers pick up maps at Tokyo railway stations, then race through congested local parks in search of checkpoints. In the United States, however, it is just beginning to catch on. The 2,000-member U.S. Orienteering Federation, headquartered in Athens, Ohio, helps organize more than 700 meets a year in which nearly 10,000 people compete.

With compasses in hand, orienteers are sent off from the starting point at two-minute intervals. Not until he or she leaves the starting line is each racer given a topographic map of the immediate area and some clues, describing the terrain

A competitor must know how to read a topographical map.

where each of the 8 to 12 checkpoints is located. Marked by red and white flags, these points also have specially coded hole punches, which the runners use to mark their entry cards. On most courses, flags are placed behind rocks or in trees, and in the most advanced category they are so carefully located that a racer must practically step on them. All entrants are timed from the starting point and the person who completes the course in the least amount of time is the winner in each category.

Eager to give it a try, I ventured to a state forest in Michigan not long ago, where the annual U.S. orienteering championships were being held over a two-day period. Though lacking in Super Bowl hype, the event had a strong air of camaraderie about it. Among the 300 contestants were business people, school kids and about 25

Marines. Nearly every age bracket was represented.

"Only about half the people here are really out to win," commented Eric Wagner, an outgoing, knowledgeable orienteer. "Most just want to have fun." Wagner was more intent on finishing off a bowl of cornflakes than preparing for his morning race. The Ohio University sociology professor was badgered into trying the sport a few years ago by one of his students. Today, he's addicted.

One man who looks capable of challenging anyone is Bob Turbyfill, a brawny 30-year-old Marine captain who is the defending U.S. men's champion. "Orienteering is a humbling sport," he says, "and in the Marines, we have a saying about how up-and-down it can be: 'Sometimes you eat the bear and sometimes the bear eats you.'" Turbyfill should know. Two years ago, while competing in a meet in Gatineau Park in Quebec, Canada, he charged through a thicket and ran straight into a mama black bear and two cubs. Though the former football star looks capable of handling almost any situation, he decided to give the bears the right-of-way and headed up the nearest tree.

Turbyfill is not the only American who has had a startling experience at sprawling Gatineau. Four years ago, Louie van Steveren, a U.S. inter-collegiate champion, got so lost there that he ran right off the course map into an area where Prime Minister Trudeau's summer home was located. Bursting through the brush, the tall, red-headed Michigan native ran straight into a trio of armed soldiers, who were patrolling the house grounds. The guards immediately turned the rifles on the startled van Steveren, who had a tough time explaining what the map and the compass were all about to the three French-speaking Canadians.

"Orienteering is a lot like playing cowboys and Indians," notes Maxine Grace Hunter, 33, a college physical education instructor from Pennsylvania. Competing in a meet in Ohio she somehow got turned around and wound up almost 5 miles (8.05 kilometers) off course. Emerging from the woods, she raced headlong into the middle of a suburban shopping center and had to hitch a ride back to the race's starting point. "I wasn't really lost," she recalls. "They just hadn't made the map big enough."

Orienteering maps describe the terrain where each of the race's checkpoints is located.

Among the orienteers, the award for the "most dramatic recovery from a potentially disastrous error in judgment" probably goes to a young Marine who ran straight off the concealed edge of a cliff. He broke his fall by grabbing onto the branches of a tall tree that grew up from the bottom of the cliff. Amazingly, his next control flag was located directly at the base of that tree.

There, about to punch his entry card was another orienteer who looked up in disbelief as the Marine came out of the sky, punched in and then disappeared into the forest.

In Michigan, fortunately, there are no cliffs to conquer and I was not required to perform any daring leaps. To make the race enjoyable for novices, the meet's sponsors had placed the first three control flags on the course in fairly obvious spots, and, on leaving the starting line, I located each in rapid succession. Finding the fourth

Orienteers use compasses to guide them on a course.

was a different matter, however. By that time, I was feeling a bit cocky and I bounded through the forest without paying any attention to the squiggly topographic lines on my map. It was a serious mistake. Without warning, I suddenly plunged knee-deep into that slimy bog and only some last-second fancy foot-work kept me from falling headlong. When I emerged a minute later, I was not only wet and embarrassed, but also totally lost.

Simultaneously, a bleary-eyed college student, wearing a green nylon suit and dripping with sweat, dashed out of the trees and looked about in a frenzy, not even slightly aware of my presence. After checking his bearings, he was gone again in a flash. Taking it as an omen, I followed him, this time using my compass and map to guide me through the thick underbrush. Sure enough, there it was: the fourth red fluorescent flag. From that moment on, I made very few moves without first consulting my compass and map.

The person most responsible for bringing this zany sport to the U.S. is Bjorn Kjellstrom, a giant Swede who, at 66, looks only half his age. Not long after the sport was invented, Kjellstrom and his two brothers became widely known as the top orienteers in Sweden, and in 1933 the three began manufacturing a compass now used throughout the world by all types of outdoor enthusiasts: the Silva. Simple to use, it combines a liquid-based compass needle with a clear, protractor-like background that, when laid atop a map, makes it easy to take a reading from one point to another.

In Michigan, precautions are taken before the championships. "We work quite closely with the state department of natural resources," says van Steveren, organizer of the meet, "to make sure that we avoid sensitive areas, and I think we've succeeded in keeping our impact down to a minimum. There are too many nature freaks competing here for us to do it in any other way."

The fact became obvious to me as I neared the end of the race. On the way to my last control point, I came upon another contestant who had stopped to watch a bright yellow bird, sitting on a branch a few yards away. "That's the prettiest warbler I've ever seen," he told me, unconcerned that a few seconds might make a difference in where he eventually placed in the meet. After chatting with him briefly, I pushed on.

Exactly 58 minutes after leaving the starting blocks, I rounded a bend and sprinted down the final corridor of trees to the finish. A small crowd of spectators had gathered around the finish line and as I crossed the tape, they gave me a rousing round of applause. Little did it matter that at least a dozen other people had finished ahead of me. What did matter was the fact that I had successfully located all eight control flags, and that I had begun to master the fine art of compass and map reading.

Who knows, now, what other challenges lie ahead of me? Christopher Columbus, out of my way!

Number of Words: 1671 ÷ _____ Minutes Reading Time = Rate _____

I. FACT/OPINION

Decide whether each sentence below taken from the selection is a fact (F) or an opinion (O).

_____ **1.** Today, orienteering is compulsory in Swedish public schools.

_____ **2.** Orienteering is a lot like playing cowboys and Indians.

_____ **3.** It's doubtful that children who take part in orienteering races will ever be lost in the forest.

_____ **4.** In some circles, orienteering has been criticized for its potential insensitivity to the wilderness.

_____ **5.** Landing on the moon was the greatest orienteering feat in history.

6 points for each correct answer   SCORE: _____

II. REFERENCE

Next to each subject listed in Column A, write the letter of the source in Column B that could give you information about it.

	A	B
_____ **1.**	Forests of central Michigan	**a.** Library or bookstore
_____ **2.**	Dates and locations of American orienteering meets	**b.** U.S. Department of Environmental Conservation
_____ **3.**	History of orienteering	**c.** U.S. atlas
_____ **4.**	Effects of orienteering on wildlife and vegetation	**d.** Science textbook
_____ **5.**	How to use a compass	**e.** U.S. Orienteering Federation

6 points for each correct answer   SCORE: _____

III. AUTHOR'S PURPOSE

Circle the letter of the best ending for each sentence.

1. The author's purpose in writing this article is to
   a. criticize.   **b.** inform.   **c.** amuse.

2. It is obvious that the author wants to
   a. warn readers against the dangers of orienteering.
   b. give details of the history of orienteering.
   c. share his enthusiasm for orienteering with his readers.

3. Part of the article's appeal lies in the author's use of
   a. amusing anecdotes related to orienteering.
   b. statistics from past orienteering championships.
   c. interviews with orienteering champions.

4. One of the things the author likes best about orienteering is the fact that
   a. winning a meet is less important than the enjoyment and knowledge to be gained from it.
   b. most events are only open to highly experienced orienteers.
   c. there are no set rules in the sport.

10 points for each correct answer   SCORE: _____

PERFECT TOTAL SCORE: 100   TOTAL SCORE: _____

IV. QUESTIONS FOR THOUGHT

Do you think it is fair to let children compete in the same meets with experienced orienteers? Why or why not?

Girlhood Among Ghosts

Maxine Hong Kingston

My mother left China in the winter of 1939 and arrived in New York Harbor in January, 1940. She carried a suitcase filled with seeds and bulbs.

I was born in the middle of World War II. From my earliest awareness, I dream again and again that the sky is covered with rows of airplanes, dirigibles, rocket ships, flying bombs, their formations as even as stitches. And I must figure out a way to fly between the shiny silver machines.

To my mother, forever Chinese, America was full of strangers. She called them, in Chinese, of course, ghosts.

For me then America has always been full of machines and ghosts—Taxi Ghosts, Bus Ghosts, Police Ghosts, Fire Ghosts, Meter Reader Ghosts, Tree Trimming Ghosts, Five-and-Dime Ghosts. Once upon a time the world was so thick with ghosts, I could hardly breathe; I could hardly walk, limping my way around the White Ghosts and their cars. There were Black Ghosts too, but they were open-eyed and full of laughter, more distinct than White Ghosts.

What frightened me most was the Newsboy Ghosts, who came out from between the cars parked in the evening light. Carrying a newspaper pouch instead of a baby brother, he walked right out in the middle of the street without his parents. He shouted ghost words to the empty streets. His voice reached children inside the houses, reached inside the children's chests. They would come running out of their yards with their dimes. They would follow him just a corner too far. And when they went to the nearest house to ask directions home, the Gypsy Ghosts would lure them inside with gold rings.

We used to pretend we were Newsboy Ghosts. In this masquerade we collected old Chinese newspapers (the Newsboy Ghost not giving us his ghost newspapers) and trekked about the house and yard. We brandished them over our heads, chanting a monotonous chant: "Newspapers for sale. Buy a newspaper." But those who could hear the insides of words heard that we were selling a miracle salve. The newspapers concealed green medicine bottles. We made up our own English, which I wrote down and now looks like "eeeeeeeeee." When we heard the real newsboy exclaiming his authentic calls, we hid, shame-facedly dragging our newspapers under the stairs or into the cellar, where the Well Ghost existed in the black water under a lid. We crouched on our newspapers, the San Francisco *Gold Mountain News,* and plugged up our ears with our knuckles until he went away.

For our very food we had to traffic with the Grocery Ghosts, the supermarket aisles full of ghost customers. The Milk Ghost drove his white truck from house to house every other day. We hid watching until his truck turned the corner, bottles rattling. Then we unlocked the front door and the screen door and reached for the milk. We were regularly visited by the Mail Ghost, Meter Reader Ghost, and Garbage Ghost. Staying off the streets did no good. They came nosing at windows—Social Worker Ghosts; Public Health Nurse Ghosts; Factory Ghosts recruiting workers during the war. (They promised free child care, which our mother turned down.)

It seemed as if ghosts could not hear or see very well. Momentarily lulled by the useful chores they did for whatever ghostly purpose, we did not bother to lower the windows one morning when the Garbage Ghost came. We talked loudly about him through the fly screen, pointed at his hairy arms, and laughed at how he pulled up his dirty pants before swinging his hoard onto his shoulders. "Come see the Garbage Ghost get its food," we children called. "The Garbage Ghost," we told each other, nodding our heads. The ghost looked directly at us. Steadying the load on his back with one hand, the Garbage Ghost walked up to the window. He had cavernous nostrils with yellow and brown hair. Slowly he opened his red mouth, "The . . . Gar . . . bage . . . Ghost?" We

"Come see the Garbage Ghost get its food," we children called.

ran, screaming to our mother, who efficiently shut the window. "Now we know," she told us, "the White Ghosts can hear Chinese. They have learned it. You mustn't talk in front of them again. Someday, very soon, we're going home, where there are Han people everywhere. We'll buy furniture, the real tables and chairs. You children will smell flowers for the first time."

"Mother! Mother! It's hap-

"Human beings do not need Mail Ghosts to send messages," my mother said.

pening again. I taste something in my mouth, but I'm not eating anything."

"Your grandmother in China is sending you candy again," said my mother. "Human beings do not need Mail Ghosts to send messages."

I must have tinkered too much wondering how my invisible grandmother, illiterate and dependent on letter writers, could give us candy free. When I got older and more scientific, I received no more gifts from her. She died, and I did not get "home" to ask her how she did it.

As a child I feared the size of the world. The farther away the sound of howling dogs, the farther away the sound of trains, the tighter I curled myself under the quilt. The trains sounded deeper and deeper into the night. They had not reached the end of the world before I stopped hearing them, the last long moan diminishing toward China. How large the world must be to make my grandmother only a taste by the time she reaches me.

When I last visited my parents, I had trouble falling asleep, too big for the hills and valleys scooped in the mattress by child-bodies. I heard my mother come in. I stopped moving. What did she want? Eyes shut, I pictured my mother, her white hair frizzy in the dark-and-light doorway. (My hair is white now too, Mother.) I could hear her move furniture about. Then she dragged a third quilt, the thick, home-made Chinese kind, across me. After that I lost track of her exact location. I spied from beneath my eyelids and had to hold back a jump. She had pulled up a chair and was sitting by the bed next to my head. I could see her strong manicured hands in her lap. She is very proud of her hands, which can make anything and stay pink and soft while my father's became like carved wood. Her palm lines do not branch into head, heart, and life lines like other people's but crease with just one atavistic fold. That night she was a sad bear; a great sheep in a wool shawl. She had recently taken to wearing shawls and granny glasses, American fashions. What did she want, sitting there so large next to my head?

"What's the matter, Mama? Why are you sitting there?"

She reached over and switched on a lamp she had placed on the floor beside her. "Aiaa," she sighed, "how can I bear to have you leave me again?"

How can I bear to leave her again? She would close up this room, open temporarily for me, and wander about cleaning and cleaning the shrunken house, so tidy since our leaving. Each chair has its place now. And the sinks naked in the bedrooms work, their alcoves no longer stuffed with laundry right up to the ceiling. My mother has put the clothes and shoes into boxes, stored in preparation for hard times. The sinks had been built of gray marble for the old Chinese men who boarded here before we came. I used to picture modest little old men washing in the mornings and dressing before they shuffled out of these bedrooms. I would have to leave and go again into the world out there which has no marble ledges for my clothes, no quilts made from our own ducks and turkeys, no ghosts of neat little old men.

"I'll be back again soon," I said. "You know that I come back. I think of you when I'm not here."

My mother dragged the Chinese quilt across me.

"Yes, I know you. I know you now. I've always known you. You're the one with the charming words. You have never come back. 'I'll be back on Turkey-day,' you said. Huh."

I shut my teeth together, vocal cords cut, they hurt so. I would not speak words to give her pain. All her children gnash their teeth.

"The last time I saw you, you were still young," she said. "Now you're old."

"It's only been a year since I visited you."

"That's the year you turned old. Look at you, hair gone gray, and you haven't even fattened up yet. I know how the Chinese talk about us. 'They're so poor,' they say, 'they can't afford to fatten up any of their daughters.' 'Years in America,' they say, 'and they don't eat.' Oh, the shame of it—a whole family of skinny children. And your father—he's so skinny, he's disappearing."

"Don't worry about him, Mama. Doctors are saying that skinny people live longer. Papa's going to live a long time."

"You're always listening to Teacher Ghosts, those Scientist Ghosts, Doctor Ghosts."

"I have to make a living."

She had taken off the Ace bandages around her legs for the night. The varicose veins stood out.

I closed my eyes and breathed evenly, but she could tell I wasn't asleep.

"This is terrible ghost country, where a human being works her life away," she said. "Even the ghosts work, no time for acrobatics. I have not stopped working since the day the ship landed. I was on my feet the moment the babies were out. In China I never even had to hang up my own clothes. I shouldn't have left, but your father couldn't have supported you without me. I'm the one with the big muscles."

"If you hadn't left, there wouldn't have been a me for you two to support. Mama, I'm really sleepy. Do you mind letting me sleep?" I do not believe in old age. I do not believe in getting tired.

"I didn't need muscles in China. I was small in China." She was. The silk dresses she gave me are tiny. You would not think the same person wore them. This mother can carry 100 pounds (45.4 kilograms) of Texas rice up and down stairs. She could work at the laundry from 6:30 a.m. until midnight, shifting a baby from an ironing table to a shelf between packages, to the display window,

Mother wore a kerchief over her nose to protect her from the ghost's fumes.

where the ghosts tapped on the glass. "I put you babies in the clean places at the laundry, as far away from the germs that fumed out of the ghosts' clothes as I could." I thought she had wanted to show off my baby sister in the display window.

In the midnight unsteadiness we were back at the laundry in a picture of domestic tranquility. Mother was sitting on an orange crate, sorting dirty clothes into various heaping mountains—a sheet mountain, a white shirt mountain, a dark shirt mountain, a work-pants mountain, an underwear mountain, a little hill of socks pinned together in pairs, a hill of handkerchiefs pinned to tags.

"No tickee, no washee, mama-san?" a ghost would say, so embarrassingly.

"Noisy Red-Mouth Ghost," she'd write on its package, naming it, marking its clothes with its name.

Back in the bedroom she coughed deeply. "See what I mean? I have worked too much. Human beings don't work like this in China. Time goes slower there. Here we have to hurry."

"Time is the same from place to place," I said unfeelingly. "There is only the eternal present, and biology. The reason you feel time pushing is that you had six children after you were 45 and you worried about raising us. You shouldn't worry anymore, Mama. All of us have grown up."

"It's a good thing I taught you children to look after yourselves. We're not going back to China for sure now."

"You've been saying that since 1949."

"Now, it's final. We got a letter from the villagers yesterday. They asked if it was all right with us that they took over the land. The last uncles have been killed so your father is the only person left to say it is all right, you see. He has written saying they can have it. So. We have no more China to go home to.

"I don't want to go back anyway," she said. "I've gotten used to eating.

"I've lost my cunning, having grown accustomed to food, you see. There's only one thing that I really want anymore. I want you here, not wandering like a ghost from Romany. I want every one of you living here together. When you're all home, all six of you with your children and husbands and wives, there are 20 or 30 people in this house. Then I'm happy. And your father is happy. Whichever room I walk into overflows with my relatives, grandsons, sons-in-law. I can't turn around without touching somebody. That's the way a house should be." Her eyes are big, inconsolable. A spider headache spreads out in fine branches over my skull. She is etching spider legs into the icy bone.

"When I'm away from you," I had to tell her, "I don't get sick. My chest doesn't hurt when I breathe. I can breathe. And I don't get headaches at 3:00 a.m. I don't have to take medicines or go to doctors. Elsewhere I don't have to lock my doors and keep checking the locks. I don't stand at the windows and watch for movements and see them in the dark."

"What do you mean you don't lock your doors?"

"I do. I do. But not the way I do here. I don't hear ghost

I am pleased to hear my mother call her pet name for me as she says good night.

sounds. I don't stay awake listening to walking in the kitchen. I don't hear the doors and windows unhinging. I've found some places in this country that are ghost-free. And I think I belong there, where I don't catch colds or use my hospitalization insurance. Here, I'm sick so often, I can barely work. I can't help it, Mama."

She yawned. "It's better, then, for you to stay away. The weather in California must not agree with you. You can come for visits." She got up and turned off the light. "Of course, you must go, Little Dog."

A weight lifted from me. The quilts must be filling with air. The world is somehow lighter. She has not called me that endearment for years—a name to fool the gods. I am really a Dragon, as she is a Dragon, both of us born in dragon years.

"Good night, Little Dog."

"Good night, Mother."

She sends me on my way, working always and now old, dreaming the dreams about the sky covered with airplanes and a Chinatown bigger than the ones here.

Number of Words: 2465 ÷ _____ Minutes Reading Time = Rate _____

I. LANGUAGE USAGE

For each sentence, circle the letter of the best meaning for the words in italics.

1. Whenever my parents said "home," they *suspended* America.
    a. left   **b.** pretended it didn't exist   **c.** meant

2. I was too big for the *hills and valleys* scooped in the mattress by child-bodies.
    a. indentations   **b.** holes   **c.** broken springs

3. She was forever cleaning the *shrunken house*, so tidy since our leaving.
    a. Part of the house had been closed off.
    b. The house seemed smaller without a large family.
    c. The house had been partly destroyed.

10 points for each correct answer   SCORE: _____

II. CLASSIFYING

Some of the sentences below refer to the mother and daughter; others refer to the grandmother. Write the letter of the correct heading before each sentence.

                    a. Mother   **b.** Daughter   c. Grandmother
_____ **1.** She continued to live in the past.
_____ **2.** She died, and I did not get "home" to ask her how she did it.
_____ **3.** She was well educated, with a broad perspective on life.
_____ **4.** She had discovered a better way of life for herself.
_____ **5.** She tried to make others feel responsible for her loneliness.
_____ **6.** She believed in modern science.

5 points for each correct answer   SCORE: _____

III. INFERENCES

Circle the letter of the sentence that best states the implied meaning of each statement.

1. To my mother, America has always been full of machines and ghosts.
   a. My mother believed that dead people walked about.
   b. She believed that only the Chinese were real people; the Americans were not.
   c. She felt that her dead ancestors were always with her.

2. "No tickee, no washee, mama-san?" a ghost would say, so embarrassingly.
   a. The Americans would make fun of the Chinese.
   b. Americans liked to tease their Chinese friends.
   c. Many American customers spoke very poor English.

3. "Time goes slower in China; human beings don't work like this."
   a. The mother remembered life in China as being more relaxed and enjoyable than her life in America.
   b. Life was so boring in China that time passed slowly.
   c. There was never enough work in China to keep the people busy.

4. "I don't want to go back anyway," she said. "I've gotten used to eating."
   a. The mother preferred American food to Chinese food.
   b. She remembered how scarce food used to be in China.
   c. Her appetite was better here than it had been in China.

10 points for each correct answer   SCORE: _____

PERFECT TOTAL SCORE: 100   TOTAL SCORE: _____

IV. QUESTIONS FOR THOUGHT

Does this story give you a feeling of the intense love between mother and daughter? Why or why not? Explain your answer.

Yesterday's

A hawk perches on the back of a giant tortoise of the Galapagos Islands as they bask in the sun.

Beasts

Tui de Roy Moore

In quiet clearings they graze methodically, their dark domes shining in the sunlight. Three to four thousand of these giant tortoises of the Galápagos bask on the grass or lumber among sprawling bushes and dwarf trees, just as they did millions of years ago. Some wallow in mud puddles, while others drink from the edges.

It is a scene of primeval splendor, and with the coming of night I always feel a sense of wonder and awe. Dozens of the ponderous creatures settle down to sleep in a shallow rainwater pond as the sun sets beyond the distant clouds. I wonder: Do those glinting reptilian eyes conceal an intelligence we cannot measure?

The setting, just south of the equator, is a collapsed volcano 4 miles (6 kilometers) wide—the Caldera of Alcedo. It makes up part of Isabela Island, the largest of the Galápagos group (off the coast of Ecuador), where I live. In this ancient land, sunk 1000 feet (305 meters) into the summit of a volcano, is the largest population of Galápagos giant tortoises still to be found. To watch them, as I have all my life, is to step back into history. They are truly yesterday's beasts.

I was two years old when my parents moved here from Belgium. They had heard just enough to realize that this was where they could lead the life they were dreaming of: free and self-sufficient. At first we lived in a tent in the humid highland of Santa Cruz Island, and my earliest memories are filled with the haunting calls of seabirds that nested around our encampment. Later, my parents built a small house of lava block near the seashore. I grew up there and received my schooling at home, but most importantly I learned to look at nature and its secrets.

My interest in biology grew naturally from these early enchantments. I learned much about the ecology of the animals and plants around me from books and from discussions with visiting scientists. Over the years I have made many expeditions and stayed for long periods with my family in some of the more remote parts of the archipelago. Of these islands, one of my favorites will always remain Isabela.

In prehistoric ages, giant tortoises were widely distributed on various continents of the world, but only two populations have survived. One is here, and the other is on a small atoll in the Indian Ocean. Precisely how these landgoing creatures spanned the seas to end up on these shores will probably always remain a mystery. But when they finally did arrive, they found a land devoid of both competitors and predators. Eventually, they inhabited almost all of the Galápagos Islands.

At Alcedo the altitude ensures enough rainfall to produce plentiful plant growth. The tortoises graze on it, and during the rainy season, which lasts about three months, they stir into great activity, feeding and wandering, drinking from murky ponds and mating. This is the time, too, for aggression. At chance meetings, individuals face off and raise their heads high, jaws agape. Usually the smaller tortoise backs down, but sometimes the attacker will ram it to hasten its retreat.

Later in the season, as the rains subside, so does the activity in the area. The females begin searching for adequate nesting sites. Some travel many miles before digging a circular cavity in a patch of firm soil where they lay as few as 3 eggs or as many as 25. These they spread gently with their stubby hind feet and then cover them with an even layer of dirt, leaving the eggs to be incubated by the warmth of the sun. Four to six months later, the tiny young dig their way to the surface and begin a life of their own.

Whatever the season, tortoises are terribly curious. Once, while I was sitting under a tree eating lunch, a loud metallic clang made me look to where I had hung a large aluminum pot about 4 feet (1.2 meters) off the ground. A large, startled tortoise was hurriedly retracting into his shell with a violent hiss. As I watched, he rose again and, stretching his neck to the maximum height, attempted to take a bite out of the bottom of the pot. Again a loud clang, and the pot began to swing, scaring him back into his shell once more.

That was only one of many close encounters I have had with tortoises. On another occasion—during my very first visit to Alcedo, in fact—I actually climbed aboard one. I disapprove of this domineering practice, yet on this occasion the temptation was irresistible, and I was compelled to give it a try. It was late afternoon, and several males were begin-

A young tortoise accompanied by its mother.

Preserving the Galapagos giant tortoise is a major challenge.

ning to bed down in a muddy wallow.

Slowly I followed one, resting my weight on his shell as he walked along until gradually I lifted my feet off the ground. For the first few steps he was slightly off balance, but he quickly adjusted and continued into the puddle unaware of my presence. As most of the sleeping space was already taken, my tortoise then proceeded, bulldozer-like, to ram the others out of his way, making little of the extra 150 pounds (68 kilograms) he was carrying. Finally he settled down in the thick mud, scraping with a blunt foot at a tick attached to his rough neck. Gently I reached out and began scratching for him. He apparently enjoyed it and extended his neck further, but turning his head, he saw my silhouette and quickly pulled in his head.

For countless thousands of years, these great creatures lived undisturbed on their Ecuadorian islands. But in the last three centuries, people have exerted an ever-increasing pressure on them. Although there were no permanent human settlements on the islands until about 150 years ago, early whalers and pirates took away vast numbers of tortoises as a handy supply of fresh meat that could be stored alive for months aboard their ships. Once, nearly 75,000 tortoises existed on the islands. Now there are only 10,000 at most.

But the most severe impact came from the introduction, both deliberate and accidental, of many domestic mammals turned wild. On some islands goats, donkeys and cattle compete for food and may trample the tortoise nests. On others, pigs, dogs, cats or black rats eat the tortoises at various stages of their development.

It was not until 1959 that Ecuador, which owns the Galápagos, took action. That year the government set aside all uninhabited areas in the islands as its first national park. Slowly conservation programs were set in motion, and today, despite a chronic shortage of funds, operations have been set up to eliminate or control certain animals and to breed some tortoises in captive conditions for repopulation programs.

The results have been successful in some cases, but many actions remain to be launched. One thing is clear: Preserving the Galápagos giant tortoise and trying to restore its natural habitats will take many more years and at times will present major problems. Our hope is that someday large numbers of these domed giants will again graze or browse silently on islands where they have long been decimated.

Number of Words: 1207 ÷ _____ Minutes Reading Time = Rate _____

I. INFERENCES

Put a check ✓ next to three ideas that can be inferred from the selection.

_____ **1.** The author's parents were not pleased with their life-style in Belgium.

_____ **2.** The author found living in Ecuador an enlightening, enriching and enjoyable experience.

_____ **3.** The land of the collapsed volcano is a dangerous place.

_____ **4.** Giant tortoises are brazen and annoying.

_____ **5.** Many times people do not give thorough consideration to the possible effects of their actions.

10 points for each correct answer   SCORE: _____

II. VOCABULARY

Fill in the letter of the correct word: a. prehistoric, b. archipelago, c. uninhabited, d. humid, e. curious.

1. I stayed in some of the most remote parts of the _____ .

2. At first we lived in a tent in the _____ highland of Santa Cruz Island.

3. In _____ ages, giant tortoises were widely distributed on various continents of the world.

4. Whatever the season, tortoises are terribly _____

5. That year the government set aside all _____ areas in the islands as its national parks.

6 points for each correct answer   SCORE: _____

III. CAUSE/EFFECT

Each set of sentences contains a cause and an effect. Put a C next to the cause and an E next to the effect in each set.

_____ **1.**   The giant tortoises flourished and eventually inhabited almost all of the Galápagos Islands.

_____   For the tortoises, the Galápagos Islands were devoid of both competitors and predators.

_____ **2.**   Many feral animals have been introduced to the Ecuadorian islands.

_____   Only 10,000 of the 75,000 tortoises remain.

---

10 points for each correct answer   SCORE: _____

IV. STORY ELEMENTS

Put a check ✓ next to four words that describe the mood of this selection.

_____ **1.**	informative	_____ **5.**	hostile
_____ **2.**	satisfied	_____ **6.**	respectful
_____ **3.**	thrilling	_____ **7.**	exciting
_____ **4.**	awed	_____ **8.**	hopeful

---

5 points for each correct answer   SCORE: _____

PERFECT TOTAL SCORE: 100   TOTAL SCORE: _____

V. QUESTIONS FOR THOUGHT

Do you think that humanity can continue to progress without interfering with the balance of nature? Why or why not?

IMMORTALITY

Robert Henderson

On a Wednesday morning in February, a man by the name of Martin Gaines left his sprawling apartment on Murray Hill, stopped at his office on West Forty-fifth Street, and went on a business trip. Between then and the time he returned home on Friday evening, several things took place more or less at random, and settled down to lie in wait for him.

On Wednesday afternoon, Ellen, his wife—a composed, habitually smiling woman of fifty—picked up at her hairdresser's a magazine abandoned there by a girl who had bought it to read an article about Swedish glass. In it, Mrs. Gaines read an article about pernicious anemia. Her secret and baseless conviction had long been that her body, round and firm as it was, could never last out the natural term of a life as wonderful as hers. Compen-sation would surely set in. By nightfall, symptoms were at her, and by Friday, though still smiling, she was stiff with fear. On Wednesday night, Martin's son Steven quarrelled with his girl (who had just finished quarrelling with her sister) and stayed out in sorrow until four o'clock, cruising the city in the family car. In the morning, his mother forbade him the use of the car for a week. Being seventeen years old, he found his fate unacceptable, and, after lying elaborately about where he was going, took the car out again that night and banged it up. And on Friday afternoon Martin's married daughter, Leora—pregnant, and anxious for the sake of her child to have what belonged to her—called on an aunt, her father's sister, to claim a pair of candlesticks she believed her grandmother had left her. The aunt, who believed, or wished to believe,

that they had been left to her, refused Leora, who grew angry, and promised to appeal to her father for justice that very night.

Of course, Martin Gaines knew of none of these matters when, returning, he reached his office toward dark on Friday. Even so, he was reluctant to go home; what he did know was that his father would be there overnight. His father was lame from a broken knee suffered the year before, his blood pressure was a standing cause of family alarm, and he had no business on earth living alone in his old house in New Jersey. This Martin was going to have to say to him, as he had said it before, being duty bound. He would have to insist that his father sell the house and move to the city, where his children could keep an eye on him. There would be an argument.

So Martin stayed longer in his office than he need have. He telephoned his wife, and was struck by the dull tone of a voice that habitually welcomed him home from a two-day trip with the gladness owed to someone back from war. When he questioned her, she told him only about Steven and about Leora. Martin shook his head, knowing that that was not all that was the trouble. He washed, still delaying, but accepting the whole responsibility for putting things in order when he did get home.

It had never in his adult life occured to him that he was not answerable for everything that came to his attention. He was a tall, lumbering, sombre man, lit by occasional gleams of hopeful humor, and he lived, in a way, a little apart from his wife and children, whom he cared for deeply. He longed for them to be reasonable, honest, fair, and, above all, safe. To these ends, he was somewhat of a justice of the peace with them; if he had not been, he would have indulged them wildly.

He waited a few minutes more, staring out the window at the sky turning purple as night came. It was an effect of clouds and city that he loved. Then he saw that the rain that had been falling earlier had stopped. He rolled his umbrella into a neat foil. He emptied his briefcase and put into it papers he would not read that evening because he would be explaining to his father the hazards of age. And, having delayed that long, he reached the sidewalk outside his building in time to see a man, who had just been struck by a car, lying out in the middle of Forty-fifth Street.

The man lay on his side on the wet, glistening pavement, near the cover of a steaming manhole. A policeman bent over him. A doorman directed passing cars to the far side of the street. People had begun to gather. The man's hat and glasses had fallen off, and his overcoat lay bunched across his hips like a lifted skirt. His hair was short, neat, and lightly gray. A foot in a polished shoe was thrown out crookedly. One trouser leg was pulled up, showing a few inches of white skin. In the distorted moment, this seemed distressing to Martin; he was immensely sorry for the man who was helpless to correct it. The man was of indeterminable age—forty, fifty, no age in particular—a commuter sort of man, in tweed jacket and dark slacks, on his way to his train, going home. Blood was spreading out slowly from underneath him. The policeman took his wallet from his jacket and dug through it. One of the onlookers picked up the man's briefcase and umbrella and stood holding them uncertainly. An ambulance siren screamed far away, and then screamed nearer. Steam from the manhold blew across the man's face. Martin, who had already seen more than he wanted to see, walked away.

He put the thought and sight of the man out of his mind as well as he could, but the man

persisted in returning. His briefcase had become Martin's briefcase, and his umbrella Martin's also—or perhaps it was the other way around. Martin crossed Fifth Avenue among swarms of people, thinking it incredible that all of them should be unaware that half a block away from them a man lay alone—absolutely alone, for all the gathering crowd—in the wet street. He tried to rehearse what he would say to his father, but he could not find cheerful words. He wanted to paint the picture of a small, bright, safe apartment in the city, with the old man in it, safe from vertigo and falls. But though the picture had come to him often and clearly in the past, he could see nothing now but the man there in the street and his quiet face—the face, he thought, of an established, educated man, well groomed, a husband and fa-

ther—and the steam, and the shining pavement. The man was the sort of man to whom, surely, such things are expected not to happen. Death (and Martin was sure this was death) comes to such people in prescribed and manageable ways. It comes dishevelled in the street only to the faceless, bodiless ones, the people whose paths one has never imaginably crossed, whose addresses are on strange avenues of their own, where one has never walked—not to men just leaving the office, as on all Friday evenings of their lives, dressed like oneself and on their way to dinner.

He walked another block among commuters funnelling into Grand Central. A tall, red-faced man, topcoat flying, clutching under one arm a package merry with valentine hearts, drove himself zigzag toward some train; clearly he would be ruined if he missed it. (The man lying in the street had been tall, too, or had seemed so: this man's height, perhaps—Martin's height.) Who was waiting for the man in the open topcoat at the far end of his train ride? Probably—and Martin now found the idea both astonishing and heart-rending—it had not even dawned on him that he could conceivably not get there. And the whole station, Martin knew, was at that moment full of breakable people who were not thinking of themselves as such. Breakable people were in the stories in the newspapers they were carrying. They themselves were only going home.

Martin turned south toward his own home, as aware as he had been only once or twice in his life that he was mortal. The fact, as a simple fact, was an old, unquestioned one; mortality had always been lurking, out there at the far end. But it had seldom quietly stood by in the near distance.

Steven Gaines was in his room—a fort where he immured himself much of the time. He was making pencil sketches of his left hand when he heard his father open the front door. Steven selected two of the sketches and threw the rest away, first tearing them into minute pieces, then stirring them in among the other trash in his wastebasket. He dated and initialled the two, and put them in a folder of drawings that had a title page reading, "The Sketchbooks of Steven Gaines, Museum of Modern Art, New York, New York, 1967." He put the book in his suitcase, which he kept locked, in a padlocked compartment under a window seat. Then he set out to see his father and get it over with.

His father, too, was anxious to have it over with. He had kissed his wife, and had gone into the living room—a room that had not changed very much in twenty-five years, and one that Martin had never imagined looking otherwise than as it always did. But it occurred sharply to him now that the pictures were sure sometime to come down from the walls and not go up again, the windowpanes would sometime, somehow, be broken and not replaced. Steven came in, braced for judgment, and Martin wondered for a moment what to say—what was important enough to say. Then his mind reliably supplied the answers: it was not so much the damaged car that mattered as the lying. The car called for a penalty—a curtailed allowance. Deceit called for discussion. Martin began to discuss. The required words came, but they struck him as being almost entirely weightless.

They struck him, in fact, as being quite stupid and irrelevant, though the idea that they could be so was preposterous. He had never doubted the importance of honesty, and he did not doubt it now. What he was saying was only what was expected of him—by Steven and by himself—but that was the very trouble. He did not want to say it. He felt as if he were speaking ponderously to an inconsequential misdeed, not talking to his son. He wanted to reassure himself on the point, but he did not know exactly how to go about it. Still discussing, he put his left hand on Steven's shoulder, striking a pose that he recognized at once as condescending, though he had by no means meant it so. He had not considered at all what Steven would think; he had merely wanted to touch him, here, in their room that would sometime cease to exist.

A dozen seconds went by, and then there was a tiny movement of the shoulder. Martin dropped his hand, and went on listening to his words as they

sounded justly deploring false-hood.

When the lecture was fin-ished ("We'll say no more about it," Martin said, in con-clusion), Steven went to clean up, and Martin stayed where he was. He thought that Steven was a distant boy, a secret boy, who kept things to himself. Then the telephone rang, like a portent, and as Martin went down the hall to answer it, he thought again of the man lying in the street. Would the man's wife be setting the table, or would she know by now that he was dead? If she did not, was a telephone ringing, this minute, in the dark, high up in some echoing office (an office with a desk in it exactly like Martin's desk, chair like his chair)—ringing and stopping, and almost at once beginning to ring again? Martin picked up his own telephone. His angry daughter was calling. He said yes, of course she could come and talk to him in an hour or so.

And in her apartment in Cooper village, Leora Gaines Downey (by her married name) hung up the phone and went back to the table where she and her husband were finishing an early dinner; it was early be-cause her husband studied at night. She was a slight, graceful girl, with glasses that enhanced the seriousness of her small face. While she ate her cheese and fruit, she marshalled argu-ments in favor of her child, who would need a few modest heirlooms, and against her aunt, who had everything a lone woman could want, in-cluding candlesticks that did not belong to her, and—now that Leora thought of it—a sea-shore cottage she never used and certainly never lent. To Leora, justice was far from blind; it saw clearly through her eyes. When dinner was over, she stacked the dishes, and told her husband, to his relief, that he must not think of going with her to see her father. She put on coat and boots and a red stocking cap, and, before she left, saw that her husband was comfortably arranged with books and pencils and pipe at the cleared dining table. She kissed his bald spot, which she regarded as a fore-shadow-ing of eminence, and went out.

So now it was Martin's daughter who was talking ear-nestly about affairs that three hours before would have been of weight, and Martin was list-ening silently. And again the whole familiar process of es-tablishing what was right and what was wrong seemed to

time there in his chair and somewhere outside the room.

Then Leora paused and took off her glasses, and put them on again and looked at him, and in that instant Martin saw her as she had once stood looking at him when she was seven—tiny and owlish and dubious, but severe—showing him her first glasses. The glimpse vanished, but it left Martin filled with love for her, and with pity for her shortcomings, which did not seem to matter as much tonight as they often did. He ached at the thought that people besides himself might be aware of them, and he wanted her to have the candlesticks. But what he said to her, as if by rote, was that he would discuss the whole question with her aunt, and sort out what the case was. Whoever was fairly entitled to the candlesticks should have them. And as he said this, a queer thought ran into his head—that not only had Leora always needed him, if only to settle her disputes, but he had always needed her to bring them to him.

Ellen Gaines, her hands steady, her smile fixed, cleared the dinner table, walking with the light stateliness she had early learned to walk with. But she felt as if she were in a tight

have gone off balance, and words were being spent on trivialities. Leora had come as the family was having coffee, and while she filed her brief for the candlesticks, Martin looked around at them all—his discursive (and, he thought, rather greedy) daughter, his distant son, his troubled wife (*something* was troubling her), his stubborn father—seeing them in a strange double perspective, as if he were at the same case—an invisible garment that cramped and suffocated her, and shut out all but the mere sight of her surroundings. Through it neither love for nor pride in her silver and her Wedgwood managed to seep. Out of it, when she smiled at her father-in-law, she was sure her smile emerged a ghastly grin. From inside it, she absently waved Leora home to her husband, though Leora's husband signified little to Ellen at the moment. Inside, with her, were thoughts of hospitals and pain, and bills—enormous bills for her husband to spend his good years paying. And, to be sure, the tips of her fingers were cold, and tingling constantly, and the base of her spine felt hollow. She looked in a mirror for ravages, or at least for the bedragglement of the sick, and saw, mocking her, her clear skin, her clear eyes, the soft, perfect waves of her gray hair. She told herself brusquely that her fears were imagination, and then, weakly and ruefully, she laughed at herself for the folly of trying to pretend that she was well. And all the time she was dreading, and longing for, the moment when she would tell her husband of her fears, as she always did. He would be scornful, and

would talk about hobgoblins. He would tell her to be reasonable. He would point out that she had been examined only lately and found to be blooming. He would restrain his evident impatience, though giving her selected glimpses of it, while explaining that her symptoms were pure nerves. And at last, whether because he had said and done these things or merely because she had come out into the open with her fear and talked about it, the fear would begin to ebb, and she would feel abashed and relieved, and life and her silver would look lovely to her again.

Meanwhile, Martin had lit a cigarette and gone into his study. It was time for a television roundup of the news, and he turned it on, then turned it off. It was foolish to wonder if any notice would be taken of one man killed by a car. That was a commonplace, not a piece of news. And yet the man's life had ended there, by the steaming manhole; it had all been bound for that spot. It seemed to Martin that the block might have been shut off for a while—kept quiet—but of course such a thing was ridiculous. People were swarming along it this very minute—noisy, bound for theatres. But

he hoped it would not occur to the man's wife, wherever she was, to think how quickly his death could vanish from the street. Then Martin, putting out his cigarette, went to the kitchen to help his own wife, whom he did not want to leave by herself any longer.

He walked through the swinging door into the bright kitchen, and took a towel from a rack, and for a short while, in the warm kitchen world, his own world looked like itself again. True, he had a peculiar, a senseless moment when he saw his wife visibly there beside the sink and in the same second was stormed by a longing for her, as if she were far away. But then she told him about her tingling fingertips, and he recognized, and climbed onto, what he thought was solid ground. He spoke about morbid spells and fancies, and not giving way. She mentioned vague, terrible diseases of the blood. He went on with his curative discussion. But presently, looking tired, she dropped her work and sat on a stool, her hands folded in her lap, like a large but wholly biddable child waiting to be told what to think, and at once his sound common sense and his balance collapsed again, and he was not sure of himself. He heard himself reminding her of all the good things the doctors had said, but the indulgent, scoffing note he tried to strike was missing. She nodded with no conviction whatever, and alarm grew up in him. He told himself that there was not a chance in a thousand that she was right, and then that there was indeed just that.

So the hobgoblins crossed over into Martin, and the man on Forty-fifth Street, who had reduced the importance of other things tonight, had now reduced that of reason and common sense. It seemed to Martin that he and Ellen were standing there alone in a small pocket of light and comfort encircled and crowded by loss—not his loss of her, or hers of him (though he was appalled at the thought of ever being out of reach of her if she should need him), but all loss, all ending. And there was not time, in a mortal moment, to be reasonable. He said dutifully, hopefully, that her symptoms were pure nerves, but still he could not bring the necessary—the unanswerable—impatience into his voice. She listened, and nodded again, and went back to the sink, and Martin was sure that he had failed her.

Perhaps he had failed them all, he thought a little later, but he could not say in exactly what way, or why he thought so. He felt perplexed and thwarted. Right was right, fairness was fairness, honesty was honesty, sense was sense, and yet all these old, dependable companions seemed to be standing guard between him and his family tonight. They would not let him go close, which was all he wanted, and he guessed with a shock that perhaps they seldom had. Now it was nearly nine of this queer evening. The dishes were done. His father was in the study watching television and waiting. There were not many places for Martin to go, many things to do—many excuses for delay—in even a large apartment.

He went into the living room and tried to think of his father's house, and his father endangered in it. Nowadays, the old man forgot things, and this exasperated him, and when he found he had forgotten something, he would stamp away intemperately, upstairs or down, to do or get whatever he had forgotten. He had set up a workshop in the basement, and he was repairing half the furniture in the house. The basement stairs were steep and dim. The furniture he dragged down was cumbersome.

The house was too big, the house was too old. But the

more persistently Martin tried to reason against it, the more persistently a memory kept pressing to be recalled. In front of the house was a tree that one night long ago had been sheathed in ice and had bewitched him. It had, in fact, caused him to feel a good deal as he felt now, and when he let the memory come, he did so reluctantly, not wanting to make him compound the evening's heresies.

He and Ellen had come back from their honeymoon that night. Their apartment was not finished. They were staying in Martin's old room, and Ellen was already asleep when, past the edge of the drawn blind, Martin caught a glimpse of the tree sparkling in the light of the street lamp under it. And he did something foreign to a nature that did little on impulse and was designed, on the whole, to see icy trees as merely trees in danger of cracking. He got up and raised the blind, and the tree blazed in at him, glittering and still, and more beautiful than any tree—or anything else—had seemed to him before. He went back to bed and lay a long time looking at it, while it entangled itself in his life. Ellen beside him, and his parents in the next room, and

his childhood and his hopes, and the old house and the tree became part of one another, and all of them were suddenly, for the first time, capable of ending. The past was already gone, and the future—bright though it was, and varicolored and lovely as the tree—now also had a treasonable look of brev-

ity. But in spite of transience and loss, the spell of a moment of light that would never come again enclosed and gently, sweetly exalted him. The tree would lose its enchantment, and presently grow green again, and later storms would ice it, but he knew that that night would be unique among the nights of his life.

Now Martin went into the study and saw that, though the set was on, his father was not looking at television. He was gazing blankly down the length of his legs, stretched out in front of him. When he heard Martin come in, the old man heaved himself up and limped to the set and turned it off. He sat down and smiled hesitantly at Martin, who realized that it might not be necessary to argue, after all. The realization undid him. He knew—he allowed himself to know, though he had spent a year keeping the demoralizing knowledge at arm's length—that his father wanted beyond anything else in the world to spend the rest of his life in his own house. And Martin suddenly wanted overwhelmingly to stop trying to do the prim, trifling things he would have done on any ordinary night, and to give a gift, however foolish, however risky, to one of the people he loved.

"Well, Papa," he said, "I think we ought to have a talk about the house."

"I know how you feel about it," his father said. "I suppose you're right." His voice was lifeless.

"I don't think you'd be happy in an apartment, or in the city," Martin said, while his mind, in its rectitude, protested and retreated and protested. "I don't think I'd consider it, if I were you."

"What's that?" his father asked.

"You want to stay at home," Martin said, "so why don't you?"

"I would like that," his father said slowly. "I think I will. You're positive you don't mind?"

"No," Martin said, already dismayed. "You stay at home."

Steven Gaines, leaving the dinner table, had seen his father look at his sister with an expression that brought into relief a wonderfully fluent line of forehead, nose, and jaw. He went to his room, and after a few tries, jubilantly decided that he had caught it. He put the sketch in his folder, and set out to visit his girl. He considered asking her to marry him. He yearned to take the sketch along, but he did not; it was something to be revealed only when the time came.

Ellen Gaines, in her kitchen, had finished the dishes in panic. It seemed plain enough to her that Martin knew how ill she was; she had heard it in his voice. Then she watched his back as he went out the door, and abruptly she knew that he knew nothing—nothing at all. He was only afraid. He was afraid, without reason, for her. The panic lifted. What became plain to her now was that he needed her solace, and she felt glad and guilty. The fear of the last three days began to drain away. She wanted only to reassure him, to protect him. She resolved that she would not be so foolish again—so childish. She thought fondly that she must take better care of her husband.

Steven came hurrying through the kitchen on his way out. He kissed his mother as he passed, astonishing her; it was not exactly a thing he did every day. Heartened, she decided that she would save Martin a chore. She went into their room and called her sister-in-law. The sister-in-law laughed, and said that of course she would gladly give the candlesticks to Leora. The trouble was only that Leora had insisted that they belonged to her.

The goodness of Ellen Gaines' life flowed over and

through her once more. She called Leora and told her that she could have the candlesticks at the price of a small retreat. Seeing her child already passing the candlesticks on, with grace, to new generations, Leora planned a handsome retreat, intended so to propitiate her aunt that when summer came she would offer her the beach house. Then, looking ahead as her habit was, Leora saw herself inheriting it.

Martin's father was, by this time, on his way to bed. He reflected that if Martin had not changed his mind, he would have had to give in. Later, secretly, in the dark, he confessed to the darkness that he was not

at all certain how long he could keep the house up. Still, he was excited—too excited to sleep. He thought that one minute you could be about to live your life out in a place you'd rather be dead than live in, and the next you could be on your way home, where you belonged. Silently, he promised Martin that he would be careful on the stairs. One had to slow down a little as one grew older. But, by and large, it seemed to him that now he had all he was prepared to ask of life. He could not make out what had got into Martin, but he would always be grateful that it had.

It was now just past eleven. On a short, winding country road leading from Route 22 a few miles north of Armonk, there were three houses, well apart. In the one nearest the highway, a single bedroom light was shining, back of slanted Venetian blinds. In the second, there were no lights. In the third—all the lights were burning. At eleven-ten, an enclosed black car—a small hearse—turned off Route 22, wound along the short road, and turned in at the driveway of the third house.

Number of Words: 4918 ÷ _____ Minutes Reading Time = Rate _____

I. SEQUENCE

Number the following events from 1 to 5 in the order in which they took place in the story.

_____ **a.** The man lay on his side on the wet, glistening pavement near the cover of a steaming manhole.

_____ **b.** The sister-in-law laughed and said that of course she would gladly give the candlesticks to Leora.

_____ **c.** A small hearse turned off Route 22, wound along the short road and turned in at the driveway of the third house.

_____ **d.** Steven Gaines was making pencil sketches of his left hand when he heard his father open the front door.

_____ **e.** Martin Gaines left his sprawling apartment, stopped at his office and went on a business trip.

7 points for each correct answer   SCORE: _____

II. STORY ELEMENTS

Put a check ✓ before the best ending for each sentence.

1. The mood of this story is
_____ **a.** gay and lighthearted.
_____ **b.** somber and mysterious.
_____ **c.** exciting and scary.

2. This story could best be described as a study of
_____ **a.** family members who cannot relate to one another.
_____ **b.** how a shocking incident changes a man's outlook.
_____ **c.** a personal tragedy that brings a family closer together.

3. In this story we see the main character
_____ **a.** realize that his life is rich and meaningful.
_____ **b.** rid himself of responsibility.
_____ **c.** develop an awareness of his own mortality.

5 points for each correct answer   SCORE: _____

III. LANGUAGE USAGE

In each pair of sentences the italicized word is spelled the same, but the accent is on a different syllable. On the line before each sentence write 1 if the accent is on the first syllable; write 2 if the accent is on the second syllable.

1. _____ **a.** Steven tore the sketches into *minute* pieces.
   _____ **b.** He knew his father would be home any *minute*.
2. _____ **a.** She looked in the mirror at the *perfect* waves of her hair.
   _____ **b.** It had taken her years to *perfect* her hairdo.
3. _____ **a.** At the *present* moment his wife looked tired.
   _____ **b.** He wanted to *present* his daughter with the candlesticks.

10 points for each correct answer   SCORE: _____

IV. CLASSIFYING

Match each character in column A with his or her description from Column B.

	A		B
____ 1.	Martin Gaines	**a.**	conniving and selfish
____ 2.	Ellen Gaines	**b.**	a hypochondriac
____ 3.	Steven Gaines	**c.**	talented and introspective
____ 4.	Leora Gaines Downey	**d.**	somber and troubled

5 points for each correct answer   SCORE: _____

PERFECT TOTAL SCORE: 100   TOTAL SCORE: _____

IV. QUESTIONS FOR THOUGHT

Would you say this story had a happy ending? Why or why not?